O me of little faith

O me of little faith

TRUE CONFESSIONS OF A SPIRITUAL WEAKLING

JASON
BOYETT

ZONDERVAN®

ZONDERVAN.com/
AUTHORTRACKER
follow your favorite authors

ZONDERVAN

O Me of Little Faith
Copyright © 2010 by Jason Boyett

This title is also available as a Zondervan ebook. Visit www.zondervan.com/ebooks.

This title is also available in a Zondervan audio edition. Visit www.zondervan.fm.

Requests for information should be addressed to:

Zondervan, *Grand Rapids, Michigan 49530*

Library of Congress Cataloging-in-Publication Data

Boyett, Jason.
    O me of little faith : true confessions of a spiritual weakling / Jason Boyett.
       p.   cm.
    Includes bibliographical references.
    ISBN 978-0-310-28949-4 (softcover)
    1. Faith 2. Boyett, Jason. I. Title.
  BV4637.B69   2010
  234'.23—dc22
                                           2009051034

Published in association with the Anderson Literary Agency Inc., 435 Convent Avenue, Ste. 5, New York, NY 10031. Giles Anderson (212) 234-0692.

Cover design: Curt Diepenhorst
Cover photography: Steven Wohlwender
Interior design: Michelle Espinoza

Printed in the United States of America

---

10 11 12 13 14 15 16 /DCI/ 20 19 18 17 16 15 14 13 12 11 10 9 8 7 6 5 4 3 1

To my grandparents,
John and Mary Boyett and John and Cleta Brown,
who despite incredible hardships have maintained a strong,
inspiring faith and passed it along to the rest of us.

Contents

Acknowledgments

O*Me of Little Faith* is a new kind of book for me. It is much more personal and far more story-driven than my previous work and therefore stretched my writing in many good ways. But it also made me nervous. Doubt can be a tricky subject, especially among religious readers. *Was I getting this right? Did I explain that clearly enough? Does that metaphor work?* (Especially the turtle thing.)

To answer those questions, I relied on the feedback of a number of close friends — writers, editors, and fellow doubters — and the best parts of this book ended up with these readers' fingerprints all over them. I want to thank Cara Davis, my very first editor and an early advocate of my writing, to whom I legitimately owe much of my career; my old high school friend Matt Gulde, a religious-minded deep thinker who asked hard questions of my first draft and reminded me that the bench-press bar was 45 pounds; my brother, Brooks, and sister and brother-in-law Micha and Chris Hohorst, all of whom set the standard for a well-reasoned, well-lived faith; and other friends like Jeremy Courtney, Angela Hart, Matthew John, Justin Shumaker, and Matthew Paul Turner, who read and commented on early drafts and encouraged me along the way.

I also want to thank Darrell Anderson and the EXP community in Amarillo, who allow me to speak on occasion despite my spiritual uncertainty, and where the seeds of this book were planted during a talk I gave in 2008. Because of the hard work of my agent, Giles Anderson, this idea ended up in the capable hands of the team at Zondervan. I am especially grateful to Angela Scheff, whose editorial brilliance and admiration for Kierkegaard made the finished product so much better.

Most of all, I am grateful to my family. This book is dedicated to my grandparents, who have given us Boyett kids a deep legacy of faith — one I am doing my best to continue. My parents, Mike and JoDeane Boyett, have been ridiculously supportive of my career, even when I write things that might make them uncomfortable. My in-laws, Dick and Beverly Storseth, break all the bad stereotypes about in-laws and love me unconditionally — and not just because I provided awesome grandkids. And I hope those awesome kids, Ellie and Owen, will someday read this book and understand why their dad said "that's a good question" more often than he gave a good answer.

The Doubter's Road

I am a Christian. I have been a Christian for most of my life. But there are times — a growing number of times, to be honest — when I'm not entirely sure I believe in God.

There. I said it.

So now you know, and we can both relax and talk about it. Confessing the presence of spiritual uncertainty in my life is a relief. I can breathe easier now because I don't have to pretend. I don't have to hide my conflicted feelings when we talk about Jesus and the Bible. I don't have to feel like a jerk if you, or anyone else, look to me as some kind of spiritual expert or teacher. I don't have to tiptoe around the word most of us hesitate to use in church or around Christian friends because it freaks us out so much.

Doubt.

Now that it's out in the open, I can strip off my happy Christian mask, climb down from whatever pedestal I've hoisted myself up on, and be who I really am: a committed follower of Jesus who occasionally finds himself wondering if maybe, just maybe, we've made this whole thing up.

Let's back up for a minute though, because there will be plenty of room in this book for me to talk about myself. What I want to discuss here, at the beginning, is you. Let's talk about what's going through your head right now. I have a feeling you might be thinking one of two things.

The first is this: *He's not sure he believes in God? The last thing I need to read is the navel gazing of some self-absorbed, relativistic, weak-minded writer who struggles with faith. If you have so much trouble believing in God, dude, why don't you quit writing books and start reading the Word? (You might start with James 1:6.[1]) Pray or something, but quit blabbing about it. It's bad enough that you're questioning your own faith. Don't pull us down with you!*

Is that your response? If so, that's fine. Don't worry about it, because it's not unexpected, and I totally forgive you for calling me "weak-minded." Also, I admit to being "a wave of the sea, blown and tossed by the wind," as James so colorfully puts it. I'm not especially proud of being a doubter. Like treading water in the ocean during a tropical storm, it can be exhausting, uncomfortable, and fairly dangerous—but I'm not going to pretend that it doesn't have some redeeming qualities.

Nor am I going to get defensive. You're a little mean,

---

1. "But when you ask, you must believe and not doubt, because the one who doubts is like a wave of the sea, blown and tossed by the wind" (James 1:6).

perhaps, but not entirely wrong in wanting me to shut up so I don't mess up the current quality of your belief. I don't want to do that. So if you are rock-steady in your faith and have no interest in reading a book about doubt, then by all means, put this one down. Put it back on the shelf. Walk away slowly and enjoy your blessings. Firm faith is a gift. I'm happy for you — I wish I could *be* you.

But I'm not. Which brings us to a second potential reaction to my doubter's confession. It's one of recognition and relief: *I completely understand about the doubt thing. What you're going through? Same here. I have doubts, too. Big ones. I try to ignore them, I try to fight against them, and I try to pray for more faith. But no matter what books I read or what sermons I hear, I can't get rid of these doubts.*

If you identify with me, keep reading. Maybe we're on the same road and we can walk together. It's not the straight, easy road to faith. It's no smooth interstate highway with well-lit rest stops and clean restrooms and lots of gas stations. It's not always purpose-driven. It's not the road where the driving comes with a great soundtrack — a crisp satellite radio connection to the Almighty.

Nope, ours is the doubter's road. It's a winding, weird back road that never seems to get anywhere fast. This road is poorly lit, cratered with potholes, and far from flat. Every once in awhile it steers up into the mountains, where the air is fresh and the views are spectacular. But mostly it unwinds its graveled way through valleys, across deserts, and past sketchy small towns. The soundtrack of God's voice crackles on the A.M. band through speakers that have seen better days.

It's far from boring, of course, and eventually we may even reach the same destination as those on the faith superhighway. There's a lot to be gained by taking the road less traveled, but this is one scenic route that rarely gets recommended.

You know what it's like. You've doubted in the past. Maybe you're wracked with uncertainty right now. Or maybe you're preparing for the future. You realize that your faith — while active and vigorous today — is nevertheless fragile. At this point things are moving along nicely, but you can't guarantee they'll stay this way. If something terrible happens, will your faith survive? Will you cling to Jesus when your headlights barely brighten the road ahead and all you hear is static?

I've had the opportunity to speak about my journey of doubt at colleges and churches and in small groups, and I'm always surprised at the number of people for whom the topic is deeply resonant. "Thank you for being honest about this stuff," people say. They're usually whispering, and they lean in like they're about to tell me a secret.

"Actually, I feel the same way you do. Almost all the time. It's good to know I'm not alone."

Although the number of open skeptics in our culture is growing, doubt is verboten among most Christians. Nearly all of us struggle with doubt, but few of us are willing to own it—even though its indigo thread is woven throughout the biblical narrative. Abraham dealt with God's absence. Sarah laughed at God's slowness to fulfill his promises. Job struggled to understand God's action. David expressed his doubt in poetry. "How long, O Lord?" he asks in Psalm 13. "Will you forget me forever? How long will you hide your face from me?"

And that's just the Old Testament. In the New Testament, John the Baptist doubts whether Jesus really is the Messiah. Peter's uncertainty causes him to sink beneath the waves. Nicodemus is clueless about what Jesus teaches him, and Thomas won't believe what he can't touch with his own hands.

If we're honest, we identify with these biblical characters: sometimes God seems pretty distant. So why do we pretend otherwise? My tendency is to act as if God's apparent vanishing act is something I should be ashamed of. It's a weakness to overcome, I tell myself, a sin to avoid. So we wrestle, like Jacob, in the middle of nowhere. Isolated.

But I'm not alone, and neither are you.

That's comforting. In a church culture where we clean ourselves up on Sunday mornings and go to church decked out in smiles and wrinkle-free clothes, it's good to remember that life is messy. Some of us smell bad, and we're wearing the same jeans we spilled coffee on yesterday. Our prayers are not particularly "powerful and effective" (James 5:16). Our lives don't seem victorious. Our struggles are hard, and sometimes we're barely holding it together. Is this faith thing even worth it?

Those of us on the doubter's road are constantly good at one thing: asking questions. Whether we ever find the answers or not, the questions are always there — and not just questions about whether or not God exists. Have you ever asked any of these questions?

- What if religion and our longing for God is just the way our brains are wired? Could spirituality just be the product of chemistry or electrical impulses?
- What if the atheists are right, and faith is just a crutch we've developed to give life meaning and mitigate the specter of death?
- Is there any real difference between the ancient religious stories of Judeo-Christianity and the folklore of, say, Norse or Greek mythology? Or even the Flying Spaghetti Monster?[2]

---

2. See www.venganza.com if the FSM parody is new to you.

- Are the New Testament stories about Jesus trustworthy? How do we know it's not some big *Da Vinci Code* hoax or cover-up by a power-hungry church?

- If the Bible is supposed to be completely inspired by God, why does it seem to have mistakes and factual contradictions in it?[3] And why do the typical Christian explanations of these contradictions always seem so lame?

- Stories like God instructing Abraham to sacrifice his son Isaac, or the destruction of the Canaanites, or the whole book of Job, seem so brutal and heartless. Am I really supposed to love and serve a deity who, frankly, comes across that unattractive?

- Do I have to believe in demons and angels and all that weird spiritual warfare stuff in order to be a Christian?

- Do I have to completely disregard scientific ideas like the theory of evolution or the incredible age of the universe in order to maintain my belief in the authority of the Bible?

- Why do Christians get so weird about the "end times"? Why do some Christians get so weird, period?

---

3. I just lost a few of you with that statement, didn't I? If you're offended that I think there are some troublesome sections of the Bible, then this probably isn't the book for you.

- Why do Christians seem more interested in partici- pating in a social club than living out the basic teach- ings of Jesus?
- Why do evangelical Christians emphasize making a "personal decision for Christ" and getting people to pray a "Sinner's Prayer" when the Gospels don't really show Jesus doing either of those things?
- When we go to other countries on evangelistic mission trips, are we really making a difference in people's lives? Or are we just pushing our agendas and culture on someone else and making ourselves feel better?
- If Christians really believed their friends were bound for hell — the kind of hell where the unforgiven are tortured physically for ever and ever — wouldn't Christians do everything they could to get them "saved"? Then why don't I?
- Why do some Christians focus so much energy on policing the culture and so little on producing it?
- If some Christians really are able to heal people, why are they putting on big conferences — and making people come to *them* — rather than hanging out in cancer wards or visiting the sick?
- Are huge worship centers and gymnasiums and fancy youth buildings a natural extension of Jesus'

commission to the disciples to go into all the world and preach the gospel? Would the early church even recognize the way we practice Christianity now?

- When people go around thinking God is speaking to them and giving them specific directions, couldn't that "voice" just be their own imagination?

- What does Christianity look like to outsiders such as people born into Islam, or Buddhism, or some other religious system?

- If God is loving and just and concerned with the suffering of the innocent, why does he allow children to die? Why does he allow little kids' parents to die? Why does he let terrible accidents happen? Why do Christians still get cancer like everyone else? Why does anyone get cancer?

- Why does evil exist? If God created the world and called it "good," then where did evil originate?

- What if I had been born into another culture and practiced another religion with complete devotion, would God still allow me to be tortured for eternity in hell? Even though I was pursuing him, but through the wrong religious system?

- If one definition of a *lie* is "something intended or serving to convey a false impression," then why do so many pastors wear toupees, and why does no one seem bothered by this?[4]

I could go on and on. I haven't asked any questions about HIV/AIDS, homosexuality, politics, the church's response to the environment, or other hot-button issues. I haven't gotten into my questions about tithing, and how we view financial blessings, and the whole prosperity-gospel show. I haven't touched on the exclusivity of Christianity and why we sometimes have to explain away the verses that say Christ died to save everyone.

I haven't listed everything because it seems like the list is already too long. It makes me nervous to ask these questions so publicly. Maybe you've asked some of these questions too. Maybe some of them bother you. You might be scandalized or angry enough to quit reading this book.

My purpose isn't to answer these questions. I'm not a scholar or a theologian or a pastor, so I'll leave the apologetics to someone else. And to be honest, to me these aren't questions that can be satisfactorily answered by, for instance, reading a book of "answers to hard questions." I hate expressing my doubts only to be told, "Well, you should just read John Piper," or "Here, listen to these sermons by Tim Keller" (or R. C. Sproul, Rob Bell, or Mark

---

4. Sort of a silly question, I guess, but it's something I've always wondered.

Driscoll). I've heard all the arguments and seen all the flow-charts. I've been to the Josh McDowell conferences and heard Lee Strobel speak, but still somehow I keep missing the on-ramp to the faith superhighway.

So this won't be "Five Easy Steps to Get Rid of Your Doubt." No quick fixes. What I can promise you is companionship and conversation. You're not alone in this journey.

On the doubter's road, I need a friend to spell me at the wheel — and maybe you do too.

chapter 1

The Weakling in the Weight Room

When I was in seventh grade, there was one room on campus that I approached with dread: the weight room. I played on the basketball team—actually, *played* might be a bit of a stretch. I was *on* the basketball team. But as a five-foot, seventy-pound stick of a twelve-year-old, my primary position was holding down the end of the bench. On the "B" team.

Anyway, during the off-season, our coach decided we needed to start lifting weights. The first part of our weight training would be something he called "maxing out," which sounded awesome until I found out what it really meant. "Maxing out" means finding the heaviest amount of weight a person can lift in one single, clean, complete movement. It is, to a considerable degree, *not that awesome.*

I am a skinny, skinny person. Other than a few months of infant obesity, I have been skinny all of my life. My mom's side of the family is populated by healthy — and very thin — people, so I come by my slenderness naturally. I can't wear a regular men's wristwatch because the size of most watch faces make me look like I've strapped a wall clock to my arm. I was scrawny in junior high, and I am scrawny now.

Coach's plan was for us to max out on the bench press, and he let the big guys go first. They were intimidating enough already. Their deep voices and hairy legs indicated they were already members of the Puberty Club. (Alas, I had not yet received my invitation, and I was beginning to wonder whether I was even on the mailing list.) One by one, while the rest of us watched, the big guys methodically added weight to the bar — *clank ... clank.* Some of them were getting up into the triple digits, pressing 110, 120, even 130 pounds.

I thought about hiding under a wrestling mat.

I went last. Coach turned to me and asked, "Boyett, what do you weigh?"

"Sev — seventy pounds," I squeaked. (My voice hadn't changed yet.)

"We'll start with forty-five and work up to seventy," Coach said. "You ought to be able to bench at least seventy."

Let me pause here to reveal two important facts. The first is that Coach was under the mistaken assumption that a person should be able to bench at least his own body weight, because a bench press is like an inverted upside-down push-up. I dispute this idea even to this day. It just seems wrong.

You should also know that Coach didn't just choose the beginning forty-five-pound weight at random. Forty-five pounds was the weight of the empty bar.

That's right: I would start the process of maxing out with just the weight bar. No clanking weights. Just the bar. And, yes, it looked as wildly heroic as it sounds.

I lay down on the bench. My shirtsleeves slid back to reveal bony arms and nearly hairless armpits. A couple of spotters effortlessly lifted the bar from the rack. I lowered it down, said a quick prayer—*please please please let me push this back up*—and contracted every pectoral muscle fiber I had. And slowly, steadily, keeping my eyes closed so they didn't pop out of my head with the strain, I pressed that forty-five-pound bar until my quivering arms extended fully. I'd made it. Flush with relief, I breathed again.

"Nice job, Boyett," Coach said. "Add ten."

Clank. Clank.

The spotters loaded a five-pound weight onto each end of the bar. Total: fifty-five pounds. They waited until I steadied my small-boned jelly arms, and let go as I lowered the bar to my chest.

I pushed. I pushed some more. I squeezed my eyes even tighter. *Dear God,* I may have prayed, *please let there be some sort of Spirit-of-the-Lord Samson strength stored in my blond mullet.* I kept pushing. I came dangerously close, I think, to rupturing a disc. My back lifted off the bench, which is not recommended. But the bar wouldn't move.

"Help him," Coach finally said, and the spotters—I'm certain of this—rolled their eyes at each other as they used their pinkie fingers to lift the bar from my chest. I couldn't move.

"Boyett: forty-five pounds," Coach called out as he wrote it on his clipboard. His voice echoed against the brick walls and wood floors of the weight room, punctuated by my still-pounding heartbeat.

I don't blame him for what he said next, because who could resist?

"On the bench press, Boyett maxes out with ..." *(dramatic pause)* "... the bar. Just the bar."

I learned a lot during that season of seventh-grade basketball. I learned the Lord's Prayer, because Coach—a U.S.-born Hispanic Catholic—would have us kneel and say it prior to every game, in the King James Version.

I also learned (but never practiced) a variety of creative ways to curse, because Coach would typically follow the pre-game Lord's Prayer with a halftime litany of less-appropriate uses of God's name and certain other syllables. Our team wasn't very good, and his way of dealing with our constant failure was to string together as many expletives as he could fit between breaths.[1] I'm convinced the guy was a savant of vulgarity.

Back then, I learned something about myself that remains true to this day: I am weak. In seventh grade, that weakness was primarily physical. I became aware of it in the weight room, on the basketball court, and in the hallways when various members of the athletic staff kept suggesting that I would make a great equipment manager for the football team.

Now, a couple of decades later, I wonder if that weakness transferred from the outside to the inside. Some days, when it comes to faith, I can't bench press much more than the bar. I'm spiritually scrawny. I don't measure up to the power-lifters in the weight room.

When you live and work within the American Christian subculture — especially the less liturgical, more conservative, evangelical, megachurch *sub*-subculture — you hear a lot of people talking casually about the intimacy of

---

1. The cursing was typically followed by his slumping against the wall and saying, "I promised my wife I wouldn't swear today." I always felt kind of bad for him, because he broke a lot of promises — and clipboards, for that matter.

their relationship with God. The way they tell it, they get frequent, distinct impressions from the Holy Spirit. They get personal promptings from Jesus. They get very specific answers to prayer and detailed directions about even the most trivial aspects of their lives.

I've heard someone tell a friend, "I woke up in the middle of the night and thought of you, and it was definitely the Holy Spirit wanting me to pray for you right then and there." I've overheard a middle-aged woman say, "It was totally a God thing that my flight got cancelled, because I got to share my faith with the lady next to me. Talk about a divine appointment!"

I've heard musicians credit God with having written their song lyrics. I've heard businessmen give God credit for finally coming through with the promotions for which they'd been praying. I know a few people who don't hesitate to reveal that God told them to quit their jobs and go into full-time ministry.

One Sunday I overheard someone give this breathless recap of a worship service: "The Lord totally showed up in church this morning. When we got to that key change in 'Breathe,' you just knew God was moving."

You've heard this kind of talk too, maybe coming out of your own mouth. Please understand me: I'm not telling you—or them—to stop. I'm pretty sure most of those kinds of statements express a sincere and real faith in a personal God who is intimately involved in our lives. That people talk this way is not what bothers me.

The problem is that I can't describe my own faith that way. It doesn't feel right. It makes me uncomfortable. When I'm around people who do talk that way, it's seventh grade all over again.

Maybe I'm just a cynical grump. Maybe these Christians aren't spiritualizing chance, or common sense, or feelings, or inner desires by wrapping them in church talk. Maybe they're truly hearing from God. Maybe that's the experience of most Christians today, and I'm just missing out.

But the God-whispering-in-my-ear thing doesn't seem to happen for me. If I hear my conscience, I'm pretty sure that's because I'm familiar enough with the teachings of Jesus that I feel guilty when I've failed in some way. If I wake up in the night, I'm more likely to believe it's because my dog made a noise than to assume God wants me to pray for someone. (And why does God need me to pray for something so badly that he has to wake me up, anyway? Can't he just wait until morning? Or, you know, answer the prayer without me? Am I a soulless twit to even ask?)

If my flight gets canceled, perhaps it's just the result of a backlog of delayed flights thanks to a major storm some-where. I'm seriously hesitant to assume a master evangelistic plan behind flight delays, but many well-meaning Christians really do place so much value on a single soul that they have no problem believing that God whipped up a thunderstorm over the Dallas/Fort Worth airport, piled stress on airline employees, and inconvenienced hundreds of travelers for the purpose of engineering a conversation of eternal significance. My honest assessment of most "divine appointment" language is that it is self-centered. Especially if your divinely appointed evangelism is at the expense of a bunch of other people who just want to get home in time to tuck in their kids. (Right: I'm a soulless twit.)

If I feel an optimistic swell of "the Spirit" during a specific song at church, maybe it's just that music has a powerful pull on my emotions — a well-timed minor 7th tends to have that effect. Or maybe it's the sound of hundreds of voices singing in unison that gives me chills. Is there any chance that I've been conditioned, in the subtle Pavlovian anticipation of what happens at church, to view this feeling as the presence of God — as God "showing up"? (Anyway, isn't God omnipresent? Can an omnipresent deity ever really "show up" anywhere?)

Am I too skeptical? Too worldly? Not spiritual enough? Yes. Probably. Almost certainly. At church, in my home group, and in random conversations with fellow Christians, I often feel like my scrawny twelve-year-old self, barely able to lift the bar when everyone else is maxing out in the triple digits. I'm a spiritual lightweight.

Do I lack the eyes to see and the ears to hear? Is God really trying to speak to me through my canceled flight or my recent insomnia — only I'm just missing it? Sometimes I wonder. I'm full of uncertainty, but I know this for sure: these doubts aren't fun. It's a drag to feel so spiritually weak when everyone else seems strong, to feel so full of doubt when everyone else oozes faith. At church and around Christians, I'm sitting at the end of the bench while the game goes on without me.

But I love the Bible. I love the Jesus revealed in the Bible. On most days, I'm convinced that he rose from the dead and that he is who he claimed to be. I try to follow him. I try to keep his commandments. I think the life he models is the best way to live. I think the kingdom he invites me into is as revolutionary as they come. But I'd be lying if I said Jesus talked to me all the time, or that he always felt as real to me as my wife and kids do. Because he doesn't.

"Doubt" is my middle name.

Not literally, but close enough: I'm Jason Thomas Boyett.

I'm named after my dad, but we share a name with history's most famous doubter, the disciple Thomas. He didn't fit in either. Thomas's story is found in John 20.

After Jesus has died, been buried, and is resurrected, he appears to Mary Magdalene outside the tomb. Later, along the road to Emmaus, Jesus spends time with a couple of followers who don't recognize him at first. Then Jesus surprises his disciples when he suddenly appears in a room with locked doors.[2] He shows them his crucifixion wounds. The disciples believe, and Jesus breathes the Holy Spirit upon them (John 20:19 – 23). To risk making the biggest understatement in Christian history, I suspect this was an amazing spiritual experience, holy and unexpected. The room must have been saturated with "the power and the glory," to quote the prayer I learned in seventh-grade basketball.

But Thomas missed the party somehow. According to John 20:24 – 25, he wasn't there. All his friends leave the locked room rejoicing and saying, "We have seen the Lord!" and eventually they meet up with Thomas. They tell him all about their risen Savior, his still-visible wounds, the locked-room trick, and how wonderful it was.

Thomas can't rejoice with them, though. He feels confused about the whole thing. And left out. He simply can't relate to what they're saying because he hasn't experienced

---

2. I love this detail, because it's one of the few New Testament examples of Jesus using his power to do something closer to a magic trick—appearing as if out of nowhere!—as opposed to healing the sick or feeding the hungry. It feels like personal magic instead of an others-oriented miracle.

it. Are his friends drunk? Are they delusional? Are James and John trying to "punk" him or something? Thomas needs proof. He needs to see Jesus for himself and stick his finger in the wounds. He just can't *force* himself to believe something unbelievable.

I feel for Thomas. I feel *like* Thomas.

I *am* Thomas.

One of the earliest and most important deities in Roman mythology is Janus, the two-faced god of doors, gates, beginnings, and endings. He's typically shown with the two faces looking in opposite directions, which is why the month of January takes its first-of-the-year position and name from him. You wouldn't want to meet Janus in person, though—which face would you talk to? Where do you look? A conversation with Janus would be awkward.

Like Janus, my doubt is an awkward, two-faced freak. One face surveys the many ways I do and do not experience God. It's as suspicious as Thomas. It needs evidence. It wants something rational to hold onto—and sometimes rational proof isn't even convincing enough. It asks questions, but they're the kinds of honest questions that maybe all Christians ask at some point in their lives.

But there's another face, too. It's rougher, wilder, and more primitive, with a touch of the crazy eyes. It stares down a dangerous, dark path. It's not concerned with

chapter 2

Turtles All the Way Down

There are two kinds of people in this world: those who have read Stephen Hawking's *A Brief History of Time,* and those who want you to *think* they have read it.

I'm in the second group. I have the 1990 paperback edition of the bestseller by the well-known wheelchair-bound physicist. It's probably the most famous science book ever written. It has sold millions of copies, and upon its first release it spent weeks and weeks on bestseller lists. I'm convinced that it's one of those books — like *Moby Dick* or the Bible — that lots of people own and act like they've read, but they totally haven't.

That's how it is with me, because I keep Hawking's book on my bookshelf. I like it when people visit my home and stop by my alphabetized shelves and get to the *H* section and say, "Oooh, Stephen Hawking," as if they too are big fans.

I once tried to actually read the book, but only got to the middle of the second chapter, where the illustrations begin. Figure 2–1, "An example of a space-time diagram," features several dotted lines racing from the moon to some old-looking satellites. It has something to do with movement and relativity. It totally confused me. Figure 2–2 was even more inscrutable and lacked even the mitigating presence of the satellites. So I stopped reading.

I am not one of those people who have read *A Brief History of Time*.

But I did read far enough to encounter one of the best religious illustrations I've ever read, and thankfully Hawking put it in the very first paragraph of chapter 1. (This allows me to say things like, "In *A Brief History of Time*, Stephen Hawking tells this great story about ..." which makes people think I've read the whole book. It's genius.)

So, in *A Brief History of Time*, Stephen Hawking tells this great story about a prominent scientist (possibly Bertrand Russell) who is giving a public lecture on astronomy. He explains the movement of the earth around the sun and discusses how our sun is but one of an unfathomable number of stars in our immense universe. When the lecture ends, a little old lady approaches the lecturer and tells him that all that stuff about the planets and solar system and stars is plain rubbish. "The world is really a flat plate," she tells him, "supported on the back of a giant tortoise."

The quick-thinking scientist then asks, "What is the tortoise standing on?"

"You're very clever, young man, very clever," the old lady replies. "But it's turtles all the way down!"[1]

I can't think of a better metaphor for faith than "turtles all the way down."[2] It's memorable, because who doesn't enjoy the image of a bunch of turtles stacked up on each other? Can't you visualize them? A tower of identical box turtles, serenely stacked in an endless snaking pile. Starlight reflects from countless shells in space. A few turtles in the pile are slowly rotating, because the hard curve of the lower turtle's shell acts as a pivot point for the turtle above it, so by twitching its stubby little arms and craning its neck just enough, a resourceful turtle can start spinning like a green reptilian top. Since they're in space, the spinning never ends. It's eternal. A turtle can get a really good spin going in a weightless vacuum.

Got the picture? Now follow the twisty line of space turtles to the bottom. Does the line ever end? What do you see?

In my imagination, I see nothing. Just one last turtle, floating there in the empty, cold universe. This turtle is a little bigger than the others, maybe a little older. Definitely stronger. He's the turtle of turtles. All the other turtles

---

1. Stephen Hawking, *A Brief History of Time* (New York: Bantam, 1990), 1. That's right: page one.

2. I know the brilliant Gordon Atkinson of www.reallivepreacher.com has made the Hawking-Turtles-Faith connection before, and I'm sure others have as well.

support each other, but nothing is supporting him. He's just … there. Inexplicably. The first turtle, at the bottom of the stack, supporting the weight of all the turtles and the flat earth above him.

Now for the metaphorical reveal: The world at the top is me. Each turtle is a specific presupposition of my faith. All of these presuppositions stack upon each other until they get down to the first turtle, the one supported by nothing but starlit emptiness and space. That first turtle is the foundational belief behind everything: that God exists.

My entire spiritual self rests on that belief. Basic morality. The way I treat people. The way I raise my family. My career path. The books I write. The doctrines I hold about the Bible, Christianity, and the world around me — *all* of these things balance on that first turtle.

When I began writing this chapter, I offered up a quick, reflexive little prayer to God: *Help me get this right.* It was sort of a selfish prayer — I might as well have prayed, *Jesus, make me a good writer* — but it was honest. In making that prayer, I was acting on several interlocking beliefs, or turtles, if you'll allow me to keep calling them that. One was the belief that prayer works. It's the idea that somehow, by praying what I did, God will help me do a good job communicating whatever it is I'm doing with this chapter.[3]

---

3. Apparently the whole thing hinges on metaphorical turtles, so I need all the help I can get.

That belief rested on another belief, which is that one way to pray is by merely thinking something rather than speaking it aloud. Both of those prayer turtles stand on a still lower turtle, the idea that God not only hears my prayers — even the unspoken ones — but occasionally acts on them.

My act of praying activates a whole series of turtles, all the way down, stacked in a logical chain. Without a beginning, philosophers would call this an infinite regress. Every link in the chain depends on the next link.

But my turtle chain has a beginning. At the base of my beliefs about prayer is that first big turtle: that the God I'm praying to exists at all. He's the first element of faith, the foundation of the turtle tower. And he's supported by ... nothing. He floats in space. He's not supported by other turtles or celestial scaffolding or any sort of foundation. He's held up by mystery. That's why the question of God's existence is the biggest question of my life and yours. What if everything rests on the back of a turtle whose existence is impossible to prove?

Now is a good time to discuss Dr. Seuss.

You were half-expecting the good Doctor, weren't you? (Please say *yes*.) How can anyone describe a cosmic stack of turtles without a Yertle shout-out? If you recall the story, Yertle is an arrogant little snot, but he's got initiative. He fancies himself the "king of the pond," and as the king, he enlists a bunch of other turtles to stack themselves up into his personal throne. The other turtles comply and begin building. Yertle climbs to the top of the pile, hoping to see more of his kingdom and rise above everything else.

But he's not satisfied. He demands that the turtles stack themselves even higher, so he can be as high as the moon. As the other turtles do his bidding, eventually the stack grows too high and too unwieldy. The poor turtles at the very bottom — including the bottom-most one, an unfortunate working-class turtle named Mack — get antsy. It's not long, of course, before the weight compresses Mack, forcing out a pond-shaking burp. The burp makes the turtle pile quiver in a vertical chain reaction. Yertle loses his balance and tumbles back into the pond.[4]

The higher your turtle stack gets, the more important that first turtle becomes. Everything depends on it. Can it bear the weight? Can it sustain the pressure? How long until it burps and the whole thing comes tumbling down?

How do I know God exists?

What's at the bottom of my stack?

Have I really just spent four pages talking about turtles?

Faith is a challenge, because what it rests on — the existence of God — is hard to prove.

Let me rephrase that. It's *impossible* to prove.

I've said it already, but it's worth repeating here: I am

---

4. Dr. Seuss, *Yertle the Turtle and Other Stories* (New York: Random House, 1958).

not an apologist. I'm not the guy to turn to if you want all the logical reasons why God exists. If you're looking for ammunition to load up against your atheist friend, stop looking at me and instead sit at the feet of Ravi Zacharias or Os Guinness.

The more I struggle with my own faith, the less impressed I am with rational arguments — whether for or against the existence of God. It's my opinion that most people don't get debated into the kingdom. If the techniques of door-to-door Mormon missionaries don't convince us to join *their* church, why do we expect to convert nonbelievers with a similar approach? Could a well-meaning Muslim neighbor persuade you to switch teams with a good argument in favor of Islam? My guess is no. People are drawn to faith by our love or by the grace of God. Not by our logic.

But I'm aware that many Christians disagree with me on this, and the history of Christianity is full of proofs, theories, and hypotheses for those needing a foundation for their first turtle. Consider the following:

The Ontological Argument. Beginning with early theologians like Anselm of Canterbury and continuing through later philosophers like René "I think, therefore I am" Descartes and Alvin "I am not an old, dead guy; in fact, I still teach at Notre Dame" Plantinga, the ontological argument has a lengthy history. The basic idea here is sort of mind-blowing in a late-night dorm discussion kind of way: the very fact that we can conjure up the idea of God is proof that God exists. If God is the epitome of a perfect being — if we can't conceive of anything more perfect than God — then how could that supremely perfect being lack existence? Wouldn't nonexistence nullify that perfection? And how could we even come up with the idea of perfection if not for the existence of something perfect? Since we can think of God, we have to conclude that God exists. At the very least, we have to concede that it's rational to believe in him. Also: whoa.

The Transcendental Argument. The existence of morality and ethics points to the reality of some higher, ultra-ethical absolute. Without such an absolute, why would we humans — operating within the evolutionary rules of natural selection and survival of the fittest — all agree with each other that things like murder or genocide are wrong? The book of Genesis indicates that we're created in the image of God, so maybe that's why we all share a sense of right versus wrong and good versus evil. That standard has to come from somewhere, so maybe it comes from God. If God doesn't exist, the transcendental argument insists, then neither does morality.

The Teleological Argument. The complexity, order, and apparent purpose in nature seem to indicate a designer.

Aristotle, Augustine, Aquinas, and other important thinkers whose names don't necessarily begin with an "A" have
all floated this theory to various effect. Probably the best-
known analogy connected to it is that of the watch and
watchmaker, popularized by nineteenth-century theologian William Paley. It states that you don't look at something so complicated as a shiny new Breitling and assume
it just came into existence randomly, all on its own. You see
it and know, intuitively, that there is a craftsman behind it.
Same goes for the world around us. It's so crazy complex,
Someone must have made it.

The Anthropic Argument. This is the "fine-tuned
universe" theory, and behind it is the idea that, physically,
the universe seems to be specially calibrated for carbon-
based, oxygen-breathing humans to live in it. Miniscule
changes in dozens of different constants — from the light
transmission qualities of water, to the tilt of the earth's axis,
to the ratio of electron to proton mass[5] — would make life
impossible on our planet. Or in our solar system. Or in our
galaxy. Or at all. Take those constants and tweak them ever
so slightly, and we're gone. It's as if Someone knew we were
coming and set the table just so.

---

5. Don't ask me to explain what "The ratio of electron to proton mass" means.
All I know is it's important, because if this ratio changed even a little bit, your
body would dissolve into a gluey pile of molecules.

These are all fine arguments, and most days I think they make a lot of sense. But it also must be said that each of them has plenty of critics who also make a lot of sense. They're poking and prodding at these "proofs" for God's existence, making sure I'm aware the ideas aren't as solid as I'd like to think. In fact, some of these arguments have philosophical holes big enough to drive a truckload of atheists through.

For instance, plenty of philosophers over the centuries (including Christians like Thomas Aquinas) have found the Ontological Argument to be useless and illogical, because who ever decided that existence equals perfection? The Transcendental Argument doesn't fare much better, because the existence of an absolute sense of morality could very well be the result of evolution. What if it's little more than a shared psychological trait, adapted and refined over millions of years from one generation to another, independent of God?[6] Skeptics debunk the Teleological Argument by pointing to snowflakes, which seem intricately designed yet are formed by the natural, random physical process of

---

6. For instance, neurobiology researchers announced in late 2007 that they had directly identified "mirror neurons" in humans, specific types of brain cells that until then had only been inferred. Some trumpet the existence of these neurons—which allow us to "share" the feelings of others and are responsible for emotions like empathy and compassion—as the answer to the question of how human altruism could survive evolution. *The Moral Animal* by Robert Wright (New York: Vintage, 1995) is a compelling look at this topic.

water vapor turning into ice crystals while falling through clouds. It's not like God is in his heavenly workshop, folding up big sheets of ice paper and cutting cool snowflake designs and then shrinking them and flicking them off his workbench and onto our ski resorts like a Divine Snowmaker.[7]

And just for kicks, let's discuss criticism of the Anthropic Argument. In the physics world, cutting-edge string theorists have proposed the existence of multiverses, which is possibly one of the coolest things I've ever tried to wrap my brain around. These skeptics wonder if, maybe, there are an infinite number of universes, each containing an infinite number of worlds, each featuring an infinite number of characteristics. Infinity, as you might expect, covers a lot of bases. The logic of infinite variations means there could be parallel universes that produce planets exactly like ours, only on one earth the people have wings instead of arms and flutes instead of noses; and on another, monkeys are the dominant creatures instead of people; and on another, weak, skinny writers from Texas are revered as the essence of masculinity.

What it also means is that at least one of these worlds is going to have exactly the right conditions for life to develop

---

7. Richard Dawkins famously disputed the teleological argument with his book on evolution, *The Blind Watchmaker* (New York: Norton, 1986).

as we know it. And guess what? That's the world we live in! We're already here! No need for deities!

These rebuttals are all fine ideas, but that hasn't stopped still other philosophers from rebutting the rebuttals. Contemporary thinkers like Michael Behe and Alister McGrath poke holes in the arguments of the skeptics.[8] And so it goes, ad infinitum, until we end up here: (1) All the existence-of-God arguments make sense, even to someone like me who doesn't have the patience for especially deep theology. (2) But the refutations of those arguments *also* make sense, even to someone like me who doesn't have the patience for especially deep science. (3) Lather, rinse, and repeat steps one and two until the dance makes you dizzy.

God is hard to prove. God is hard to disprove. The existence or nonexistence of God is unprovable.

Our five senses are pretty much useless in the search for God. Though many people claim to have experienced God in a tangible way, most can't see, hear, touch, taste, or smell God. We haven't been able to get God on camera or make him appear in a laboratory. For a loving Creator who supposedly wants to communicate with his creation, God sure is hard to locate.

Apparently, that was the reason Bertrand Russell, the

---

8. See McGrath's book, *The Dawkins Delusion: Atheist Fundamentalism and the Denial of the Divine* (Downers Grove, IL: InterVarsity, 2007).

scientist from the turtle story, refused to believe in God. There's a great anecdote about his ninetieth birthday party. As the story goes, a female acquaintance approaches Russell at the party. They make small talk, and she mentions that he is not only the world's most famous atheist but also, at that point, one of the world's oldest. Then the lady asks a bold question: "What will you do if it turns out you were wrong? What if, when the time comes, you should meet Him? What will you say?"

Thrilled by the question, Russell's eyes light up. He points a bony, wrinkled finger toward the sky and says, "Why, I should say, 'God, you gave us insufficient evidence.' "[9]

Bertrand Russell had a point. We may come up with some evidence for the existence of God, but none of it is unimpeachably solid. None of the proofs that have been suggested for God's existence — or his nonexistence — are convincing enough to make much of a difference either way. Will we find one someday? I'm not holding my breath.

In John 3, an important religious figure named Nicodemus comes to Jesus at night — in secret, under cover of darkness — to talk. You get the feeling he's sneaking in the back door, trying to meet with Jesus on the sly. But to his credit, Nicodemus starts the conversation right. He

9. Al Seckel tells this story in the preface to *Bertrand Russell on God and Religion* (New York: Prometheus Books, 1986), 11.

acknowledges that Jesus is a great teacher. "No one could perform the signs you are doing if God were not with him," Nicodemus says (v. 2).

You expect Jesus to reply with something encouraging like, "Very well said, Nicodemus." Or, "You're a good man to realize this, Nicodemus." Or, "Thanks."

But no, Jesus is in a cryptic mood, so he goes all non sequitur and says, "No one can see the kingdom of God without being born again" (v. 3).

It's not in the Bible, but Nicodemus's next statement is, "Say what?"

We've ruined the phrase "born again" by turning it into an easy, step-by-step, pray-this-prayer-and-you're-done approach that a lot of us have come to understand as the minimum entrance requirement to heaven.[10] Reading this passage, though, you get a sense that Jesus isn't really talking about saying a magic prayer or going to heaven when you die. What he's doing is making a really mysterious declaration out of nowhere. Nicodemus gets confused. He asks whether he needs to exit his mother's womb a second time, as an old man. The conversation has just taken a really weird turn.

And then Jesus launches into a monologue about what it means to enter the kingdom of God and what it means

---

10. Lots more about this in the next chapter.

to be born again. His speech does little to clear up the confusion.

"You should not be surprised at my saying, 'You must be born again,'" Jesus tells Nicodemus. *Okay, so the "born again" thing is totally out of the blue. I'll give you that, Nicodemus, but what do you expect from someone sent by God? Now strap in, because I'm about to get* really *deep.*

Jesus continues: "The wind blows wherever it pleases. You hear its sound, but you cannot tell where it comes from or where it is going. So it is with everyone born of the Spirit" (v. 8).

Here's Jesus in a one-on-one conversation with an influential religious leader. We're told Nicodemus is a member of the Jewish ruling council, and Jesus has the chance here to get a powerful person on his side by describing to him what God is like. He's with a willing student, a sincere seeker, and he's been asked what it means to be born again. What does it mean to participate in the kingdom of God? What is this kingdom like? What is God like?

Jesus' answer: Wind. Being born again is like wind. The kingdom of God is like wind. The Spirit himself— God's presence on earth—is like wind.

Thanks, Jesus. That clears it right up.

I live in the Texas Panhandle, home to tornadoes and dust storms and days where the wind blows fifteen miles per hour and we call it a gentle breeze. I know wind, and this is why Jesus frustrates me with his explanation to Nicodemus. Because you can't see or hear wind. You can always feel it, of course, but only when it's in the process of passing you by. It never stays in one place. It resists being found. You can't capture wind.

My friend Steve is a meteorologist on the local news station, and he knows much more about wind than I do. He can tell you that wind is really gas particles bouncing off each other. He'll tell you about the jet stream, and adjacent air masses, and low-pressure systems meeting up with high-pressure systems, and all these other atmospheric activities that cause the flow of wind. But he can't tell you why tornadoes sometimes smash every house on a block but one. Or why a violent microburst will come out of nowhere to knock over a single building on a cloudy but otherwise windless day. He'll be the first to acknowledge that we can't really see wind; we only see the effect it has on the world around us. We feel it blow our hair and watch it flutter leaves, but the wind itself remains invisible.

Steve the meteorologist will be quick to admit: Wind is a mystery.

To Nicodemus, Jesus admitted the same: God is a mystery.

Mystery makes me uncomfortable. My tendency is to

try to explain it away. That's why I love the old philosophical principle called Occam's Razor. (And not just because the very name sounds like a cosmic weapon wielded by a Norse demigod: "Behold, mere mortal, the Razor of Occam!" It's like the Hammer of Thor, only sharper.)

Occam's Razor was a standard suggested by a fourteenth-century Franciscan friar named William of Ockham.[11] The rule is this: The best explanation for any phenomenon is the simplest one. Make as few explanatory leaps and assumptions as possible. In other words, keep your stack of turtles from getting too high.

For example, consider the conspiracy theories swirling around the assassination of John F. Kennedy, still a mysterious event. Some people believe JFK's death came at the hands of a vast CIA conspiracy involving multiple shooters, government turncoats, anti-Castro Cuban exiles, and members of the Mafia. However, a lot of assumptions must be made for the conspiracy theories to be true — not the least that so many U.S. government officials were not only in league with criminals but guilty of treason. Occam's Razor debunks the conspiracy theories and gives the simplest answer to the question *Who shot JFK?* It was Lee Harvey Oswald, a deranged gunman acting alone.

---

11. In case you're confused, it's sometimes called Ockham's Razor. But "Occam" has fewer letters, so obviously it's the preferred spelling.

Just as skeptics use Occam's Razor to discredit conspiracy theories, atheists and agnostics often apply it to religious beliefs. And even though William of Ockham was a religious man, things get squishy if you use his razor when it comes to faith. Let's be honest — explaining the universe by attributing its existence to an all-powerful Creator requires some significant steps of faith. In fact, I sometimes wonder if it needs more steps than the opposite approach. Atheism assumes we're alone in the universe and life is no more than a bunch of protons and electrons whizzing around. No divine Watchmaker. No heaven or hell. No existence after death.

But monotheism assumes an omniscient, omnipresent Creator behind every aspect of the universe, from the laws of physics to the nature of time to physical things like galaxies and tectonic plates and butterflies. The Judeo-Christian tradition assumes that this all-powerful deity remains involved in the lives of his creatures and loves them. Christianity assumes that this deity loved us so much that he entered into creation in order to communicate his love for us. And two thousand years later, a bunch of people go to church every week as a way to acknowledge it.

See? It gets complicated. Occam's Razor doesn't exactly prove the nonexistence of God, but it leans in that direction. Wouldn't it be simpler to *not* believe?

On some days, my answer is *yes*. Believe in an all-powerful Creator who is supposed to know, and love, all seven billion people on earth, including me? Believe in an all-powerful Creator who entered his creation as a helpless baby, conceived within an unwed teenager? Believe this baby grew up to be a powerful preacher and healer whose greatest enemies were religious people and whose followers were prostitutes, lepers, fishermen, and repentant tax collectors? Believe that this so-called Jewish Messiah, who was supposed to liberate his people from the oppressive Roman regime, instead taught about turning the other cheek, serving others, and showing mercy to the poor? Believe that this revolutionary, who hinted that he was divine and promised salvation, would get himself killed by the very people he'd come to save? Believe that this executed dead man only stayed dead for three days, until he came back to life and appeared before dozens of his followers? And that the misfits he had been teaching were the forerunners of a religious movement that exploded out of Judaism? And that this weird little sect would not only become a religion of its own but would end up the most influential religion in the world?

I'm supposed to believe all that? It seems like a stretch. It's hard to believe in an unprovable, mysterious God. But, mostly, I do believe.

Maybe a better way to put it is that I have *chosen* to

believe. Believers and nonbelievers alike have a choice to make about their first turtles. Both camps are operating on a series of assumptions about how the world works. Atheists have chosen to base their turtle pile on the notion that we're alone in the universe, that what you see is what you get, and that the idea of God is a human construct. Based on that foundation, the atheists' stack of turtles is quite logical. They have weighed the evidence for God and the evidence against God — and in this universe, it's reasonable to suggest that both exist, in one way or another, to variously convincing degrees — and they have chosen to side with the evidence against. There's probably no God. That's their first turtle.

The number of people who have made this choice — atheists, agnostics, and the nonreligious — is on the rise.[12] A much-discussed *Newsweek* poll and cover story from April 2009 revealed that one in ten Americans now falls within that category, which has increased fourfold over the last two decades. It's easy for believers to demonize nonbelievers, but I have to admit that sometimes I identify more closely with these so-called seculars than with some of my fellow Christians.

Why? For one thing, I can respect their decision.

12. This is a good time to note that atheism and agnosticism aren't the same thing. An atheist denies the existence of divinity altogether. An agnostic, however, holds that the existence of God is unknowable, but accepts that it's a possibility. It's a softer form of unbelief. Despite this difference, in most cases I'm using *atheists* as a catch-all term to include agnostics.

Unbelief is courageous in a heavily religious culture, which ours still is. The implications of not believing—denying a God whose existence is at least a possibility—could be significant, in an eternal as well as a temporal sense.

Furthermore, many of the arguments I've heard against atheists and agnostics are arguments made out of ignorance. Believers like to say that only religious people can find purpose in life or appreciate beauty, but I have atheist friends whose lives are as joyful and fulfilling as mine—only without God. They appreciate the beauty of nature without attributing it to a Designer. They pursue love, despite the science that reduces it to a chemical reaction in the brain. We Christians often point to subjective things like love and beauty as proofs of God and faith, but I'm hesitant to do so. Had I been raised by atheist parents, the majesty and glory of nature would likely not weigh in favor of God. Neither would the existence of love or the laughter of my children. But would they still add meaning and purpose to my life? Of course.

Unbelievers I can understand. They have doubts, just like me, and have followed those doubts to their logical conclusion: the abandonment of belief altogether. I haven't been willing to go any further down that road, but I certainly recognize it. I can identify not only with their questions but with their dissatisfaction with the answers provided by religion.

Where does my dissatisfaction and doubt come from? I want to explain it in terms of my human limitations. I am a finite creature. God is the infinite Creator. Of course I will struggle to comprehend him — there are limits to my understanding, and I doubt when I bump up against those limits. That's a nice, comforting theory until I meet the spiritual heavyweights who never seem to reach those limits. Not every Christian doubts like I do. Some Christians don't seem to doubt at all.

These are the types of believers I mentioned in the first chapter who live spiritually intense lives in which God, from their perspective, seems continually active and present. A new customer shows up out of the blue? God wants to bless their business. A random encounter with someone unexpected? God brought that person into their life for a reason. A song lyric or Bible verse gets stuck in their head? God must be trying to tell them something.

It simply doesn't occur to them that some things — like seeing an old friend at the coffee shop — happen by chance, which is typically how I would describe it. Or that there's science to explain why certain songs or phrases get trapped in a mental loop and stick there all day long.[13] These super-believers' lives are so full of God that there's no room for

---

13. Memory researchers call this a "cognitive itch" — the mental equivalent of an itchy spot on the skin.

doubt. They rarely ask questions, and when they do, the answers are not the findings of science. The answers are supernatural. The answers are usually the same: *God*.

God is rarely my go-to explanation. On the contrary, my life is so full of doubt that I can't find room for God. Does that make me a bad Christian? Am I a bad Christian because I *do* ask hard questions? Am I a bad Christian because explaining every detail as "God at work in my life" seems like religious narcissism instead of profound faith?

I don't know. I honestly don't know.

My mother worries that I think too much. She knows I struggle with these questions, but she doesn't understand where they come from. Most of the questions I ask have never occurred to her. To her my faith must seem ridiculously complicated, filled with challenges and arguments and skepticism. And she's right. We have different personalities. Our brains are bent in different directions. She had the same religious upbringing that I had (more on that in the next chapter), but we are not alike. For some, faith is a direct line between them and God. For me, faith is a tangled, knotted rope.

You can see my dilemma. When it comes to matters of faith, I find more common ground among atheists and agnostics than I do with doubt-free Christians. But I still believe. Given the choice between the turtle stack of faith or the turtle stack of atheism/agnosticism/unbelief, I choose faith, despite my doubts.

Why? Mainly, because I hope. "Faith is being sure of what we hope for," the author of Hebrews wrote, "and certain of what we do not see" (11:1). I'm not exactly "certain" of anything, but I'm sure of what I hope for: I hope there's something more than a dust-to-dust, grow-old-and-then-you-die material existence. I hope God exists.

I want there to be a greater purpose, and I want that purpose to be something more than the human altruism favored by the nonreligious. I hope that my life matters — not just to the people around me, but in an eternal sense. I hope I have a soul that will outlive this body. I hope there's a Creator who really does care about those made in his image and who interacts with his creation. I hope that the tragedies and problems of our world will someday be washed out by renewal, that good will someday prevail, that evil will be punished, that sin and heartache will eventually be no more.

I hope the message of the Bible is true. I hope life is more than molecules and mathematics. I hope death is not the end. That hope is why I believe in God.[14]

---

14. Here, the skeptic would counter that my religion is nothing but wish fulfillment — a landing strip for these hopes. I would counter that unbelief can also be a form of wish fulfillment. If I'm burdened by selfishness, moral failure, or the existence of evil, then the absence of God is a pretty good solution.

My friend Stephanie is an occupational therapist, and for several weeks last year she and her colleagues treated a self-assured young man with a hand injury. Every week the patient would drive up in a sleek, black compact BMW, which they'd admire through the office windows. The vehicle was impressive. None of them had ever seen a Beamer like it.

After several weeks of trying to identify the model, someone on staff finally asked the patient about his vehicle. "It's so different from others I've seen," the therapist said. "Is it a new model or something?"

The young man's swagger disappeared. His shoulders drooped. In a quiet voice, he said, "It's, um, not actually a BMW." He looked up. "It's a Honda Civic . . . with BMW tags on it. I bought the tags on eBay."

I want to believe in an active, loving, personal God, but maybe — underneath my Christian tags — I'm just not that kind of car. On a lot full of luxury vehicles, how did I end up a subcompact in disguise?

chapter 3

Are You Sure? Are You *Sure* You're Sure?

I didn't know much when I was five, but I knew about death. This knowledge of death came from two sources: church on Sunday mornings, and Jack Klugman on NBC's *Quincy, M.E.* on Sunday nights.

At the time, my little brother and I played a variety of imaginary children's games, including Batman and Robin, Cowboys and Indians, and an entirely made-up scenario called Deserted Island (possible influences may have included *Gilligan's Island* reruns and the *Swiss Family Robinson* story). Because we were boys, these games were always violent—people died all the time in our imaginations. According to our rules, when you died, you fell flat on the ground with your arms flailed out perpendicular to your body. Among the pre-kindergarten population of Amarillo, Texas, the death position was universal: the shape of death was a "T."

Except one Sunday night on *Quincy, M.E.* I watched a guy take a bullet on the stone steps of a fancy courthouse-type building. A van pulled up, shots were fired, and the man was fatally wounded. A splotch of blood appeared on his shirt. But he didn't die correctly. He clutched his chest and crumpled to the steps in a heap. He was not on his back. His arms were not outstretched. This was strange.

Quincy, the medical examiner played by Jack Klugman, arrived on the scene. "He's dead," Quincy proclaimed, and I learned something important about death: People don't always die in the shape of a "T."[1] But Jesus did.

I knew a lot about Jesus, too, when I was a kid. He had long dark hair and a beard, he wore sandals and a white robe with a blue sash, and he liked children a lot. In the pictures on the walls of my Southern Baptist Sunday school classes, he always had at least one happy kid in his lap and one holy hand stretched out to the rest of the children as if inviting them in for a side hug. Jesus was super nice. Jesus wanted us to go to church and obey our parents. Jesus loved us even when we were bad. In fact, Jesus loved us so much that he died on a cross to save us from our sins.

Even as a boy, I was well aware that I was a sinner. One of the first Bible verses I ever memorized was Romans

---

1. That's pretty much the only death-related thing I remember about *Quincy*, which is weird, because the whole show was about, you know, a *medical examiner*.

3:23 — "For all have sinned and fall short of the glory of God" — and it was clear that I fell squarely within that category of *all*. Maybe I hadn't killed anyone, like Cain, or Moses, or Darth Vader did, but I had disobeyed my parents. I'd been mean to my brother. And there was this kid, Greg, at my table in kindergarten who used to fold his eyelids up so you could see their slimy pink insides, which was gross. It made me happy when Greg got sick and missed school. I didn't like Greg very much, and I was sure that didn't make Jesus too happy with me.

Clearly, I was a sinner in need of salvation. This point was reinforced each week by my pastor. His tenure at our church lasted from years before my birth until my sophomore year of high school, which means he was the single pastoral influence of my childhood. He was an old-school evangelist from the Billy Graham mold, with an artfully shaped black pompadour, the quivery-deep crescendoing cadence of a southern preacher, and a knack for turning any biblical passage into a call to become a Christian.[2] Salvation had three key components:

It was a personal decision. Salvation wasn't something anyone could choose for me. Not my parents, not my Sun-

---

2. Let me say this before we go any further: I loved my pastor and still respect the man deeply. He was so much a part of my childhood that he almost seems like a distant grandfather to me. His health has declined in recent months, and the thought of his eventual death saddens me.

day school teachers, not even God. Jesus was knocking on my heart's door, I was told, but he was a gentleman. He would not break down the door. He was waiting for me to invite him in, and that was a choice I had to make on my own.

It involved a specific kind of prayer. This prayer was identified by several different titles: the "Sinner's Prayer," the "Prayer of Salvation," or, more colloquially, "asking Jesus into your heart." As I understood it, this prayer had a few requirements. You had to confess that you were a sinner. You had to believe that Jesus died for your sins. And you had to ask Jesus to come into your heart and become Lord of your life. When a person did those things — when you prayed this prayer and really meant it — then Jesus would indeed come into your heart. The result? Salvation from the wages of sin and a ticket to heaven, because . . .

It had a clear purpose. The purpose of salvation was to gain entrance to heaven after you died. Moreover, it would keep you from going to hell. This was important.

Heaven was where I wanted to go. It was a place with streets of gold and pearly gates and mansions of glory. It was a place where we would join the saints around the throne, worshiping God forever and ever. Yay!

Sort of. Golden streets and glorious mansions? I liked my own house on Lynette Street, with my bunk bed and my dog, Scuppers, and my Lego space sets. And for a kid, singing songs *forever* to God sounded about as appealing as a church service that never ended, ever.

But if the sweet by-and-by didn't seem quite as sweet as perhaps it should have, it was certainly better than the alternative. As much as I learned about heaven, I learned twice as much about hell. And I was afraid of hell.

Every week, we were reminded that hell was a real place, far from the love of God. Worse, it was filled with fire — literal burning fire — where flames scorched your body all day and night and never ever stopped. If you ended up there, you would burn for all eternity with no physical or mental relief. Hell was filled with people who had never trusted Jesus as their Lord and Savior, who had never asked him to come into their hearts. They were Chinese people who worshiped false gods, Communists who didn't believe in God at all, and Catholics who thought going to church would save them. Even my friends at school were bound for hell, destined to eternal torment if they had not invited Jesus into their hearts. I was hell-bound too, because until I made my own personal decision to follow Jesus, I was rejecting God right along with them. All of us were passengers on the speedboat to hell.

There was only one problem: I was too shy to climb out of the boat. Every church service closed with what we

Baptists called the "invitation." The congregation would stand to sing a hymn — "Just As I Am" was a favorite, as was "I Have Decided to Follow Jesus" — and sinners were encouraged to leave their seats and "walk the aisle" to the front of the sanctuary, where they would meet with a counselor, pray the Sinner's Prayer, and announce their decision to the church. Everyone would rejoice. The next week, the new believer would be baptized to start the service. It was a very public process. It scared the living hellfire out of me.

Every week, I got nervous when we reached the invitation. Every week, the pastor invited us to repeat the Prayer of Salvation after him: *Dear Lord Jesus, I confess that I'm a sinner. But I believe that you are the son of God and you died on the cross to save me. Please come into my heart, Lord Jesus, and forgive me of my sins. I give you my life and want to live for you forever. In Jesus' name, Amen.*

Every week, the pastor indicated that he knew there was someone in the congregation, someone who could feel God tugging at the strings of his heart, someone who was hesitating to take that step of faith. In my mind, clearly, that someone was me, held back by my shyness. My hands would turn clammy. My heart would pound so loudly that I'd hear it in my ears. And subconsciously I'd always find myself starting to repeat the prayer after the pastor. But I'd always stop before I got too far into it. I'd squeeze my mind shut to keep the words from forming, to pop them like bubbles before they became real.

I just wasn't ready. I wasn't ready to give my life to Jesus. The public nature of it — the highly visible sinner's walk down the aisle, the presentation in front of the church, the baptism — was almost as scary to me as the prospect of burning in hell. Stand up there in front of 800 people? Not me. Not yet. Not when I was only five years old, or six, or seven.

I very much preferred to just stand there and sing, even though I knew this was the wrong choice. Even as a kindergartener, I understood the pastor's message. I knew what was required to get to heaven and bypass hell. And I knew that every Sunday was my chance to seal my eternal fate — and an opportunity I might not have again.

"Don't put it off," my pastor would say. "Don't gamble with your soul. You could get hit by a bus on the way home from church today, and if you die without Jesus, do you know where you'll spend eternity?"

Oh, I knew all right. I'd spend it in hell. Because I was a scaredy cat. During each week's invitation I'd put off the decision, telling myself I'd do it the next Sunday. This always brought some relief until fear took over when we piled into the car to head to lunch after church. What if we got hit by a bus on the way there? What if we had a terrible car wreck? What if I died in my sin? I distinctly remember making myself pay close attention to other vehicles during these after-church drives. That way, maybe, I'd realize ahead of time when we were about to have an accident, and I could invite Jesus into my heart in that split-second before death. I knew the words to the Sinner's Prayer by heart. Could I get them recited in the seconds before I died? I thought maybe I could, and then I'd squeak into heaven.

I know what you're thinking. *What a pitiful childhood you must have had! What a wretched little death-obsessed kid you must have been!*

Looking back on it now, it does seem a little ... sad. Little boys shouldn't spend their years so fearful of hell that they're mentally planning a near-death conversion every time they get in the car. But this weekly death-hell-salvation drama sounds worse on paper than it really was. I was generally a happy kid. Great parents. Big extended family. Fun vacations. Plenty of friends. Wonderful schoolteachers.

There was just one problem, really: I grew up believing that a "decision for Christ" was the most important decision I'd ever make — only my naturally introverted personality kept me from making it. For four long years I attended church every Sunday, bearing the eternally heavy burden of spiritual procrastination. It followed me like my own little black rain cloud.

I finally stepped out from under that cloud in April of 1983, when I asked Jesus to come into my heart. Then everything got better. And I owe it all to my brother.

I was in third grade, and Brooks was two years younger. He came home from church one day and said he had invited Jesus to come into his heart. This made our family very happy, and we began talking about how he would go down to the front of the church the next Sunday morning and make that decision public. I knew this was my big chance. I was too chicken to "walk the aisle" alone, but Brooks and I could go together. So one day that week, after school, I sat down by myself on the living room floor. Twiddling a handful of cat's-eye marbles left on the carpet from an earlier game, I bowed my head and prayed the prayer. I knew it by heart.

Dear Lord Jesus, I confess that I'm a sinner . . .

I thought I felt something as I prayed — a swelling sensation in my chest, a flutter of butterflies — and I figured that was Jesus taking up residence. Then I told my parents. "When Brooks walks down the aisle on Sunday," I said, "I'm gonna go with him. I asked Jesus to come into my heart, too."

And that was that. On Sunday morning, Brooks and I walked the aisle together. I prayed with one of the counselors, who happened to have been my adored second-grade teacher. She cried a little. I cried a little, too, out of relief. We were going to heaven. *I* was going to heaven. Finally, I could ride in the car without worrying that an errant driver might sideswipe my soul into eternal fiery damnation.

Two weeks later Brooks and I were baptized, and life was good. It lasted five months.

Ask me to name the most psychologically harmful tradition of the conservative Southern Baptist church culture of my childhood, and you won't have to wait long for my answer: revivals. And all-night youth lock-ins. But mostly revivals.

Revivals were week-long evangelistic efforts where a special guest preacher (usually a professional traveling evangelist) was brought in to lead church services every night for a week. That's right: *every* night. And guest preachers are incapable of preaching sermons of manageable length, so you can imagine how exciting this was for us kids. *Revivalism* was the unspoken mindset behind these events. It had one goal: get people saved. To produce decisions for Christ, preachers would get worked up. Pulpits were pounded. Brows became sweaty. Hellfire was threatened. Stories of sin and redemption were told, all for the purpose of leading listeners to the point where they would feel the need to (1) walk the aisle, (2) pray the prayer, and thereby (3) give their lives to Jesus.

Be assured that emotional manipulation was a major factor in pushing people toward this decision. Numbers were — and unfortunately still are — important in many churches. On the first night of the revival week, we were always told that Brother So-and-So, our guest speaker, had seen many hundreds or thousands of people come to Christ as a result of his powerful preaching. Brother So-and-So was fully aware that his livelihood required keeping his numbers up, so he needed the Spirit to move. That's a lot of pressure, especially when you're relying on the part of the Godhead that even Jesus admitted was a mystery. Clearly, Brother So-and-So needed some tricks to get the party started and the Spirit moving.

One of the ways he did this was by preaching hard about the need for salvation and making us feel guilty about all the things in our lives that *didn't* save us. And he wasn't talking about bad things, like drinking alcohol or looking at dirty magazines the across-the-alley neighbor of your friend used to toss in the dumpster.[3] No, Brother So-and-So was talking about even the good things we'd do — things like attending church, or going to Sunday school, or reading the Bible. It wasn't enough to just believe in God or attain faith gradually. We had to make a personal decision

---

3. Just a random, weirdly specific example off the top of my head. That's all. Nothing more.

to follow Jesus. We needed a moment in time to look back on and say, "That's when it happened."

Examples were frequently given of people who thought they were Christians but really weren't. Brother So-and-So would tell of old church ladies who, in their eighties, realized they had never made a proper profession of faith. We learned of Sunday school teachers or deacons who, after years of faithful service, couldn't really remember a time they had chosen to follow Jesus, so they "prayed the prayer" as adults, just to make sure. The revival preachers made it clear that some Christians *thought* they were Christians but weren't really Christians after all. They had been baptized, they had walked the aisle, they even lived as followers of Jesus. But somehow, their salvation wasn't real. They needed to "get saved" the right way. They needed to pray the prayer again, to really nail it down. Good thing Brother So-and-So was there to help them.

In September of 1983, the year I prayed the prayer and walked the aisle and made the decision that would spare me from hell, I learned that maybe my salvation wasn't so certain after all. We were having a revival. It was a midweek church meeting. I was sitting with my family in our church's balcony. During the invitation, the preacher listed reasons some people mistakenly thought they were really saved. "There are some of you here," he said, "who walked

the aisle but never really turned from your sin. You con-
fessed, but you failed to truly repent. You're stuck in your
wicked ways." (*Not me*, I thought. I was only eight. My ways
weren't all that wicked yet. I checked that one off the list.)

"Some of you have attended church your whole life.
You believe in God. You believe in Jesus, but you never
truly made him Lord of your life." (*Not me. I made Jesus
Lord of my life back in April.* I'm still good.)

"Some of you prayed the Prayer of Salvation—maybe
you walked the aisle at church, or at Vacation Bible School,
or at a Billy Graham crusade—but you didn't do it of your
own accord. You did it for someone else. You did it because
a friend did it. You did it to please a family member. That,
my friends, won't cut it."

(*Uh-oh.*)

Suddenly my entire conversion was thrown into doubt.
I'd waited forever to become a Christian, and the only reason I finally had the guts to make that decision was ... well,
was it because my brother did it? I didn't know. I couldn't
exactly remember. What if I didn't make the choice "of
my own accord"? What if I did it of my brother's accord
instead? Was I even saved? Was Jesus really in my heart?
Was my whole salvation experience a sham?

The security of my eternal destination—which
had been blissfully solid for less than half a year—was

shattered, and for the next ten years I doubted my salvation. That's right: the next decade. During every revival, during every altar call, during every evangelistic emphasis, the preachers in my church insinuated that, while I might *think* I was saved, I very well could be deceived. Some of my friends gave their lives to Jesus multiple times, just to be sure. Some of my friends' parents even decided they had never been saved.

And me? I constantly wondered whether or not my prayer of childlike faith had worked. I worried that I hadn't said the right words in the prayer formula—after all, I had done it alone, reciting the words myself on the living room floor. What if I didn't truly repent of my sin? What if the condition of my heart wasn't right? What if I'd pledged my life to Jesus only because my brother had done so first? My late childhood years and all of my teenage years were plagued by those *what if*s.

I grew up in church. I loved God. I loved Jesus. I *knew* Jesus. But I was terrified that Jesus didn't know me.

By the time I graduated from high school, I'd spent almost my entire conscious life plagued by spiritual doubts. I didn't doubt the existence of God or the reliability of the Bible or anything that foundational—not yet, anyway—but I wasted a lot of mental and emotional energy doubting whether or not I was saved.

I got better, though. It happened toward the end of high school.

Somehow I got my hands on a cassette tape of Rich Mullins's *The World as Best as I Remember It* (Vol. 1), and I was enthralled, not just by the music — Rich introduced non-Appalachian Christianity to the beautiful hammered dulcimer — but by the lyrics. He wrote about Old Testament stuff like the crazy love story of Jacob and Rachel, and the even crazier talking-donkey story of Balaam, and about the quiet presence of God everywhere. Something about that album captured me in a way that music never had before, and I became a Rich Mullins fan.

In his interviews and occasional columns for a Christian music publication called *Release Magazine,* Rich wrote about that quiet presence of God and the way it appeared in our world in the least expected places. Through his influence, I encountered Brennan Manning's book *The Ragamuffin Gospel,* which first released in 1990 and rocked my spiritual world for the *next* ten years. Manning introduced me to writers like Henri Nouwen and Frederick Buechner and Robert Farrar Capon, thinkers who wrote out of the deepest streams of the Christian faith, confident in God's mercy and immersed in the "furious love of God" (as G. K. Chesterton once described it).

I started reading their books like a crazy person. And it *was* crazy. I was in high school, a time when my friends were partying and preparing for college and doing teenager stuff, and here I was, reading religious books. But these writers—Mullins, Manning, Nouwen, Buechner, Capon, and others—were speaking to me of an alien Christianity. It was unfamiliar and new, and it was like nothing I'd heard before. It was deeply spiritual. It was encouraging. It was unconcerned with the Sinner's Prayer but drenched in Jesus all the same.

They wrote about grace.

Sadly, at the time, grace was practically a foreign concept to me. It's never a good thing when a kid who has grown up in church—who has been exposed to hours and hours of sermons and Sunday school lessons and Bible studies—suddenly becomes aware, in his late teens, of the central element of the faith he has supposedly been practicing.

What is grace? I've often heard it defined, by well-meaning evangelicals, using the acronym "God's riches at Christ's expense." G-R-A-C-E.

I think that's dumb. As if the English word describing a profound concept first written about in Greek can be captured by cutesy wordplay. I prefer Philip Yancey's suggestion that defining grace is like explaining a joke or dissecting a frog: you end up killing it in the process. "I would far rather convey grace than explain it," writes Yancey.[4]

Whimsical metaphor works too, as in Cathleen Falsani's description of grace as the "oxygen of religious life."[5] Because without it, religion suffocates. If you pin me down, however, I'd probably define *grace* with the legendary quote from civil rights activist and theologian Will Campbell: "We're all bastards but God loves us anyway."[6]

I'd sung about amazing grace. I'd surely heard the word before. But the grace of Mullins and Manning and Nouwen just exploded in my psyche, leaving the best kind of mess. God loved me. Period. Nothing I could do would make him love me more. Nothing I could do would make him love me less.

Which meant all the worrying I'd done about my salvation — whether it was authentic, whether I'd pushed the right buttons or said the right words or had the right attitude — was an utter waste of my time. If God loved me unconditionally, if salvation was not about my performance

4. Philip Yancey, *What's So Amazing About Grace?* (Grand Rapids: Zondervan, 1997), 16.

5. Cathleen Falsani, *Sin Boldly: A Field Guide for Grace* (Grand Rapids: Zondervan, 2008), 9.

6. Will D. Campbell, *Brother to a Dragonfly* (New York: Seabury, 1977), 220.

but about the work of Jesus, then my eternal destiny had nothing to do with a magic prayer. In fact, it didn't have much to do with me at all. It was a gift I'd been given. There are lots of ways to receive a gift, and I was certain I had received it.

It was at the same time that I began to realize that the so-called Sinner's Prayer, as a heavenly entrance requirement, was not entirely biblical. Jesus never spoke of salvation as the recitation of a specific prayer. Paul never spoke of salvation as a specific prayer. Salvation was a question of believing in and following and confessing Jesus as Lord. It was an event *and* a process. It was belief *and* action. It was a journey in pursuit of the God revealed through the grace and mercy of Jesus.

I realized, with deep psychological relief, that I was definitely on that journey. I'd been traveling that road since I was a little kid experiencing heart palpitations during the altar call.[7]

Because of a singer and a bunch of writers outside my safe Southern Baptist upbringing, I finally stopped worry-

---

7. Please don't get me wrong: The Sinner's Prayer may not be in the Bible, but that doesn't mean it's not a legitimate first response to God. Though it's over-emphasized in many circles, I can't completely discount the method by which thousands of sincere Christians took their first steps of faith. It's not magic, but it *can* be a verbal reflection of an inner desire to follow Jesus.

ing about hell. Looking back, I'm pretty sure I became a Christian — in the traditional sense of the word — as soon as I understood who Jesus was and what he'd done for me, way before all the stress and fear kicked in.

Crap. A better understanding of the Gospel could have saved me a good dozen years of mental anguish.

But here's the thing: it's not easy to let go of that kind of spiritual uncertainty. I stopped doubting my salvation, but doubt had become second nature in my practice of faith. As soon as I left one landscape of doubt in the rearview mirror, I drove into the next one. The bigger one. What does being sure of your salvation matter if you're not sure there's Anyone around to offer it?

One of my favorite Christian saints is St. Basil the Great, the fourth-century bishop of Caesarea.[8] If anyone in history earned a title like "the Great," it was he. Basil came from a religious family but did his best work among society's outcasts and the unreligious. He was a champion of the poor, selling his inheritance to redistribute the cash to the starving. He used it to open a soup kitchen, where he made a revolutionary point of serving both Christians *and* Jews. He worked to rehabilitate prostitutes and care

---

8. This would be a good time to plug, shamelessly, my recent book *Pocket Guide to Sainthood* (San Francisco: Jossey-Bass, 2009).

for the sick, and he ended up the patron saint of hospital administrators.

But his life wasn't all peaches and cleaned-up hookers. Basil battled against the Arian heresy and tried to reform monasticism. These efforts, along with his asceticism, eventually wore down his body, and he died from liver problems before he turned fifty. His life was hard.

His brother, St. Gregory of Nyssa, once described Basil as having an "ambidextrous" faith. With one hand he accepted God's blessings, and with the other he accepted affliction. He viewed both hands as equally important, because he believed that those polar opposites — blessing and heartache — were equal players in God's plan.[9]

I'm no Basil the Great. I'm more like Jason the Unremarkable. But I love the idea of a two-handed faith. I understand the concept of a faith that is suspended, like an electrical line, between two opposite poles. One of my poles is doubt. But my line of faith remains in place because it's tethered to the other pole — my continued reliance on the revolutionary grace that Jesus showed to sinners and outcasts and doubters.

---

9. Philip Yancey builds an excellent chapter around this concept in *Reaching for the Invisible God* (Grand Rapids: Zondervan, 2000). The chapter is called "Ambidextrous Faith."

I'm one of those. It took most of my growing-up years to figure it out, but I now realize that God loves me despite my weak faith. God loves me, and I need grace.

I needed grace when I was a scared-of-hell kid too shy to walk the aisle at my church.

I needed grace when I was an anxious teenager doubting my salvation.

I need grace now as an adult struggling to maintain my childhood faith.

I need grace now because, as Will Campbell says, I'm a bastard. But God loves me anyway, and my faith is balanced between his grace on one side and my doubt on the other. I'm learning to live in the tension between those two poles.

chapter 4

The Weight of Absence

One of the passions my sixty-one-year-old dad and I share is fly fishing. There are few activities as energizing to me as standing knee-deep in a Rocky Mountain stream trying to entice a trout with a few bits of thread disguised to look like an insect with an unpronounceable name.

We try to go camping and fly fishing as often as possible, and several times each summer we load up hours before daylight for a fast, single-day trip to the Cimarron River, four hours away in northeast New Mexico. Fly fishing is a solitary activity, of course, so when we go fishing together, we don't really fish *together*. We'll find a good spot, park the car, and then split up. One of us goes upstream. The other goes downstream. We agree to meet back up an hour or two later to drive to a new spot.

I worry a lot when I'm fly fishing with Dad. He's getting older and doesn't always show up in a timely fashion at our designated streamside check-ins. My dad broke his hip in a skiing accident in the early 1990s and now limps around on an artificial hip. This makes navigating the slick river rocks quite a challenge. What if Dad slipped and fell? What if he's lying unconscious in the river? What if he had a heart attack? What if he caught a fish, and as he reeled it in a hungry mama bear leapt out of the woods and grabbed the fish to feed her cubs, and Dad's elk-hair caddis fly ended up stuck in the mama bear's cheek ten short yards away, resulting in my father's having caught an enraged mama bear on six-pound-test monofilament? (My imagination runs wild when Dad's late.)

Of course, Dad has never once been injured while fly fishing. When he doesn't show up on time, it's either because he just forgot to look at his watch (which is annoying) or he found a really nice, productive stretch of the river and was unwilling to stop fishing (which is totally justified according to our unspoken code).

Waiting for my father is horrible. When he's late, the only thing I can focus on is his absence. My mind races. Nothing else matters. Like the father in the story of the Prodigal Son, I've got my eyes glued to the trail, waiting for that first glimpse of him. The father saw the son and rejoiced. All I want to do is relax and keep fishing.

The weight of my father's absence during these times is far more powerful than the calm and comfortable experience of his presence. That unsettled sense of incompleteness and unknowing is one of the most intense feelings I ever have. My relationship with God follows the same pattern.

I seem to have a harder time than most when it comes to identifying the presence of God, especially among the evangelicals I know who see God's direct involvement in, well, *everything*. I'd think Christian musicians would hesitate to credit the Almighty for helping with their latest hit worship song when the lyrics are trite and the music derivative, but according to them, they "couldn't have written this without God." Thanks, God. And I've heard the tech crew at church give praise when a video finally works during an important part of the service — "That was God, man, that was totally God" — when my first thought is to give at least some of the credit to Dell or Sony.[1]

Recently, my church marked its fiftieth anniversary with a weekend-long celebration, ending with a big Sunday morning worship service. The worship center was packed to capacity. The service closed with a decades-old church tradition among our congregation: members held hands across the aisles while singing the hymn "Sweet, Sweet Spirit." I watched this from the stage, behind my camera,

---

1. I have no idea who gets the credit when the computer works at atheist and/or Satanist gatherings.

taking photographs to document the moment. Twelve hundred people singing in unison. From fifteen feet away, I watched my childhood pastor leaning against his wife with tears pouring down his face. He sang at the top of his lungs.

So did I. It was a deeply stirring moment. I felt something there — a combination of joy and nostalgia and pride and hopefulness. A lot of people would identify that feeling as the presence of God. Me? I don't know.

Because I've felt that way before. I've felt the presence of intense emotion at high school pep rallies before the football game with our cross-town rivals, or during a ninth-inning come-from-behind Chicago Cubs win at Wrigley Field, or right before the encore at a Coldplay concert.

When preachers get riled up — when the words and cadence and delivery start to really *hum* — we give credit to the presence of God in their public speaking. But I've preached before. I've become passionate, and it seemed like a combination of adrenaline and crowd feedback and an exciting subject. My friend Matt, a federal prosecutor, says he feels that same passion when giving the closing argument at a trial.

I am not an emotional person. I'm an introvert. So in a Christian subculture that equates emotion with the presence of God, I shouldn't be surprised that I "experience" God less than everyone else. I do not experience God very often at church, or on retreats, or during dramatic testimonies after the mission trip, or amid the small group that meets in my home. I don't experience God while preaching or praying in front of a crowd. I don't experience God at worship conferences or while playing the drums in the praise band. I don't experience God very much at all, and I think it's because I'm hesitant to automatically equate an emotional high with the presence of the Almighty.

I wonder if something is wrong with me.

So have you ever *experienced God?* you're probably asking, wondering again whether you should be reading this book at all.

Yes. At least three-and-a-half times.

The first time, I was eighteen years old. I was sitting on a ratty old yellow couch in my parents' basement, which doubled as my bedroom. I was reading Philippians 2. You wouldn't expect it from how I've described my childhood so far — what with the raging furnace of *am-I-saved-or-not* questions smoking out my interior life — but I was sort of a cut-up during high school days. I was funny and I did well in school. I was a talented writer, a burgeoning musician, and I had a killer blond mullet.[2] I was the kind of kid who got a lot of attention from adults and who wanted a lot of attention from my peers. I didn't rebel or use drugs or misbehave, but I was what you might delicately refer to

---

2. Occasionally, it was permed. Yes: awesome.

as a self-absorbed glory hound. I was praised often for my abilities, and I soaked it up. My favorite place was in the center of everyone's attention. I was *that* kid. The jokey, obnoxious, *look-at-me!* guy.

This came to a sudden stop during my senior year, when the apostle Paul used his letter to the Philippians to punch me, spiritually speaking, in the face. That morning before school, on the basement couch, I had been reading through Paul's letter to the church at Philippi. Chapter 1 was fine, though a little heavy on suffering. I breezed into chapter 2, only to crash head-on into verse 5: "Your attitude should be the same as that of Christ Jesus" (NIV). Paul then goes on to describe how Jesus humbled himself "by taking the very nature of a servant." He made himself nothing.

If you're a religious person, you may have experienced the phenomenon of reading a Bible passage countless times until it becomes mind-numbingly familiar. Then you read it again later, and for some reason the verse detonates with meaning — personal meaning — as if heaven itself has cracked open, and dazzling light pours onto those familiar words, and they carry so much authority that James Earl Jones might as well be reciting them backed by an angelic choir and a pipe organ. It felt like that. Something inside me changed.

God got my attention that day, and I look back on it as

something like a second conversion. My first conversion, despite all the inward existential drama, was outwardly uneventful. I wasn't a bad kid. I didn't go from naughty Jason to holy Jason. But upon reading that passage in Philippians, an actual shift took place within my personality, inside and out. When I walked out of the basement that morning, I was different. I *felt* different. I spent that day intent on being more of a servant to people, looking for chances to be grateful, trying for once to give attention to others instead of demanding it for myself.

I came home that night and washed the dishes after dinner. It must have come across as very, very weird. My mom asked me what was wrong. I wasn't sure what to say. *Um, God smacked me around this morning using a verse in Philippians, and now I have to change my entire approach to life?* That seemed a bit dramatic. I mumbled some excuse about trying to be helpful. But she noticed.

This is not a very humble thing to say ... but the change was permanent.

So obviously, I'm now a perfect model of humility, submission, and gracious servanthood. Right. Actually, I'm as prideful and full of myself as before.[3] But since

---

3. The evidence for this is that I just spent a couple of pages in a book — a book about myself — writing about my own humility. I'm pretty sure a truly humble person wouldn't have done that.

that morning in the basement, I now recognize those self-absorbed tendencies and try to push them away. I'm no longer the *look-at-me!* guy. Not at all. I'm a quiet writerly type on the bumpy road toward humility and gratitude, struggling to put the needs of others ahead of my own. Not always successful, but trying.

And it happened, I'm certain, because God met me once on a ratty couch during my morning Bible study.

My second experience of God occurred much later. It was the second week of January in 2006. I'd been invited to the Dominican Republic by Tom Larson, the founder of a nonprofit organization called Healing Waters International (HWI). Like me, Tom was a former advertising copywriter who burned out on the corporate grind. Unlike me, Tom ended up creating and running an organization that was meeting real needs and changing entire communities in the developing world.

Healing Waters installs water purification systems in churches in countries like Mexico, Guatemala, and the Dominican Republic. The systems take contaminated tap water and make it drinkable. The churches then sell the water to their communities at a fraction of the price people would pay at the corner store. This unique arrangement accomplishes two significant things. First, local poor people are finally able to afford clean water, which means less disease and more money for food and other necessities. Second, the churches are given a mechanism for meeting very real needs in their communities — and HWI requires the churches to reinvest the money they earn from water sales back into their neighborhoods.[4]

I was part of a group of writers and musicians Tom had invited on the trip to observe the Healing Waters systems in action, hoping we'd catch the vision and use whatever platforms we had to spread the word. Our group included Jeremy Phillips, an employee of HWI who now runs Empower African Children; Brett Larson (Tom's cousin), a folk musician from Minnesota; Paul Leon Ramsey, a United Church of Christ pastor from Denver and the founder of the gospel-punk-performance band Reverend Leon's Revival; Brad "Braddigan" Corrigan, former drummer of the famed indie band Dispatch and a singer/songwriter and human rights advocate; and Richie Furay, a founding member of the legendary bands Buffalo Springfield and Poco, and now a Calvary Chapel pastor in Broomfield, Colorado.

If it sounds like I'm name-dropping a little, that's because I am. Seriously. It was me, Tom, Jeremy, and a bunch of people a whole lot cooler than us. On the second day we were there, we visited a squatter's community called

4. I love this organization, obviously. You can learn more about Healing Waters at www.healingwatersintl.org.

Gualey, which lines the Ozama River in the heart of Santo Domingo. To call Gualey a "slum" is an insult to legitimate slums worldwide. This place is a hellhole. It's known as one of the most dangerous neighborhoods in the Dominican Republic, a place where prostitution, gang warfare, and abject poverty circle the drain of utter human misery.

As our team walked through the neighborhood, we met the moms and dads and barefoot little kids who lived there and learned how the Healing Waters system at a nearby church was improving their lives. Thanks to the inexpensive water, one family could now afford the medicine to treat their infant daughter's stomach problems (which resulted from having drunk baby formula mixed with contaminated water). Another family showed us how the church was using its water proceeds to build them a bathroom. Soon the kids wouldn't have to squat in the alley behind their shack. These were hopeful stories, but even though the sun was shining, we left Gualey feeling as if we'd walked in darkness.

The next evening, after having visited a few other communities, our team ended up at the home of Herb and Beth Allison, HWI employees who lived in Santo Domingo. We ate pizza and seven-layer dip, and at some point Brad Corrigan pulled out his guitar. He strummed it a little. And then it happened.

Within minutes, our group was being treated to an unplanned, private, pass-the-guitar concert from four great musicians. Brett Larson played a couple of his songs, and we sang along. Paul Ramsey's baritone voice shook the walls with an *a capella* rendition of "Amazing Grace." Richie Furay — a member of the Rock and Roll Hall of Fame, mind you — performed a couple of classics and some new songs. This went on for more than an hour. Several times I got chills. Then my goosebumps got chills. Once I looked at Tom and Jeremy, and we mouthed, "Wow."

The impromptu jam session ended with Brad singing a quiet, acoustic version of "Daggers," one of his best songs. When it was over, he said, "That's the first song I didn't write." He told us how it came to him late one night in what he identified as a burst of divine inspiration. "It belongs to God," Brad said. "But I get to carry it around for a lifetime."[5]

I feel the same way about that night. The hours felt like minutes, and when it was over, we just sat there grinning.

---

5. Question: So Corrigan's God claim didn't bother you? Why don't you put it in the same category as those who credit God for trite worship lyrics and computer functionality?

Answer: For one thing, "Daggers" is creative, nuanced, and powerful — the kind of song God could actually be proud of having co-authored. Second, Brad is far from a typical Christian musician or worship leader. Third, I was in a generous mood.

No one wanted to acknowledge that the evening had come to a close. I was surrounded by a community of new friends, all of them creative, gifted, passionate, and unconventional — yet faithful in their pursuit of God. Each of them had been broken by what we'd seen the previous day. We all came from different places — the West Coast and the Colorado mountains, liberal churches and conservative ones, academia and indie rock, legitimate fame and humble anonymity — yet we all felt the Spirit settling upon us amid the singing and laughing. Quietly, like snowfall, God's presence drifted over us that night in Santo Domingo.

"We needed that," Tom confided to me the next morning. I certainly did.

My third significant experience of God took place barely a year later, and again it was in the developing world. I'd kept in touch with Brad Corrigan, and he invited me to join him on a trip to Managua, Nicaragua, where he'd become involved with a community of people who lived and worked inside the city's trash dump.

More than 1,500 people live in a place called La Chureca, a squatter's colony in Managua that borders acres of broken glass, dirty diapers, burning sewage, and diseased garbage. Entire families survive there, picking through piles of refuse to find recyclables they can sell for a few cents a day. Kids as young as four dig through the trash to earn money.

Later they learn to do other things for money, including child prostitution. These kids cope with the horror of their environment by sniffing cheap, noxious glue. When you're high on shoe glue, you forget that you're hungry. Huffing glue probably also helps you forget you're a sex worker.

Brad had been introduced to the La Chureca community not long after the Healing Waters trip. He got to know some of the kids there, particularly a young girl named Ileana, and he couldn't shake the idea that God had directed him there for a reason. Brad had an idea. It's easy to give clothes or money or medical supplies to a place like La Chureca, but what would it really look like to bring light into this darkness? How can you inject life into a place so filled with death? The answer came in something familiar to him — music.

So he called all his friends — musicians and surfers and writers and college students — and asked them to join him for a full day in a garbage dump. He named the event "Dia de Luz" (Day of Light) and formulated a plan. He and his friends would enter the dump for a day just to spend time with the people there. We would work alongside them, help them gather trash, play with their kids, smile with them, and hug them. The day would end with a big concert featuring Brad and his bandmates.

And that's exactly what we did. Someone discovered

that a few busloads of students from Vanderbilt and the University of West Virginia were also in Managua on a spring break trip that week, so Brad invited them along too. Our small team of two dozen met up with a couple hundred college kids, and we descended upon the trash dump en masse. We spent several hours with the people of La Chureca, and by the end of the day we were tired, sweaty, dirty with ash and soot (fires burned constantly throughout the dump, filling the air with acrid smoke). Simultaneously, we were broken with heartache and uplifted by the smiles of the people we met. But the day wasn't over. There was still the concert.

Brad had arranged for a flatbed truck, complete with a full sound system and generator, to be set up in the one open, relatively trashless corner of La Chureca. We migrated there as the day ended. All of us — upper-class college kids, glue-addicted shoeless children, mop-haired professional surfers, a drunk guy whose pants kept falling off, and a multicultural roots-reggae band. Braddigan played. We listened. We danced. We played ring-around-the-rosie with children *and* grown-ups. We hoisted little kids on our shoulders and hopped around while their parents laughed. We were filthy with sweat and black with smoke. I looked down at one point and my left pants leg was greasy with smeared poop (not mine).

It was heaven.

Midway through, Brad launched into "Sweet Uncertain" — a song, interestingly, about doubt — and when he got to the bridge, I had to stop dancing. He sang the words in English, "Won't you come and fill this place? Lord, come and fill this place." Next to me, another guy from our team had also stopped. He knew the song, heard the lyrics, and worshipfully lifted his hand to the sky, toward the vultures circling overhead. Both of us knew: Brad's musical prayer was being answered. My eyes teared up, and it wasn't from the smoke. Because at that moment, I knew God had indeed filled that place. He was present in the trash dump, drenching us with the grace of shared humanity and the hope of healing and the joy of community. In the ninety-five-degree subtropical heat, I shivered.

I have never experienced a holier moment than that one. If the Christian afterlife is a perpetual rock concert in a trash dump, I will be thrilled.[6]

Those are my three significant encounters with God. (There's another one — I consider it a half-encounter, a sorta-charismatic experience that took place during a mission trip to Brazil the summer after I graduated from high

---

6. From this event arose a nonprofit organization called Love, Light & Melody, which uses music and the arts to help the people of La Chureca (www.lovelight andmelody.org).

school. I'll discuss it in the next chapter, because I'm still not sure whether God was involved with it or not. I used to think so. But now, predictably, I have my doubts.)

Now it's time to play armchair psychologist. Looking back, what conclusions can I draw from these experiences? What impact did they have on my faith? Why does Brad Corrigan seem to be the Forrest Gump of my spiritual life? Let's explore.

Insight #1: There's a big chunk of time between the yellow couch and the apartment concert in Santo Domingo. Almost fifteen years. During those years I graduated from high school and college, got married, had two kids, changed jobs several times, and had my first books published. Some pretty serious life events. Where was God? Should I be a little concerned that I didn't "experience God" for that long?

Good question. I have two answers. First, it takes a lot to send my God sonar pinging. As I mentioned earlier, I'm not convinced that intense emotional experiences—and I've had several—should be automatically identified as encounters with God. Second, it might be instructive here to remember the Bible.

Consider Abraham. He was old and childless, yet God promised him that the world would be blessed by his countless descendents. We dwell on that promise, and rightly so, but forget that decades passed before it was fulfilled. It was enough time for the great patriarch to doubt God's faithfulness. In fact, as the Bible tells it, Abraham went from Ishmael's birth (at the age of eighty-seven) to his own circumcision (at age ninety-nine) without hearing a peep from God. That's a dozen years. And Abraham had the kind of spiritual life where angels appeared and God gave audible instructions. Twelve years is a long time for God to seem completely absent. I'm encouraged by that.

Insight #2: These experiences were tied to an unfamiliar environment. Or, to apply a churchy cliché, they occurred when I stepped outside my comfort zone. The Philippians encounter pulled me away from the familiar attention-seeking part of my personality and plopped me down in the unfamiliar territory of servanthood. It launched me out of my comfort zone altogether.

The other two experiences happened outside the United States, amid a level of poverty I'd never experienced before. I'm not sure what kind of specific conclusions I should draw from this — do I only hear from God during personality shifts, or while in Central America and/or the Caribbean? — but it makes sense that, for a person like me who loves his routine, stepping out of that routine might be a step in the direction of finding God.

Insight #3: I got to participate fully. Part of the routine

I just mentioned involves being, well, something of a busy-body. At most church-related events, I end up taking some sort of leadership or service-oriented role. Outwardly, it's easy to blame this on the Philippians event. As my personality has shifted in the direction of service, my automatic impulse now is to find a way to help. I like to have a task. Sometimes it's a visible on-stage role. Other times it's behind the scenes. But either way, I'm most comfortable when I have a responsibility.

That's good, right? Sure, but my busyness keeps me a step away from true involvement. At church, it shelters me from the emotionalism or piety that make me uncomfortable. It's a form of self-distraction that creates distance so I don't have to participate fully in "religious activities," for lack of a better phrase. I always work, and I like it that way.

This wasn't an option in the Dominican Republic, where my job was not to lead or serve but just to observe. I had no responsibilities during the apartment sing-along, which meant I was able to fully engage in that experience. In Nicaragua, I was documenting the event for a magazine. But midway through the concert I tired of taking notes and photographs and put my journalism stuff away. In this case, I understood that I was missing out on something profound. I lifted a kid to my shoulders and hopped into the scrum. Full participation.

Could it be that my work *on behalf* of God sometimes prevents me from really experiencing God?

The three occasions mentioned in this chapter were times when my belief in God was strong. Strong enough for me to forget my doubts, at least for a season. They are the times I believed. Between them are days and months and years when I *wanted* to believe, but I struggled. These are times like waiting for my dad to show up along the stream. My experience of God's absence is more familiar — and more intense — than my brief experiences of his presence. Maybe this should bother me, but I keep thinking of a quote attributed to the monk and writer Thomas Merton: "If you find God with great ease, perhaps it is not God that you found."

Merton's statement echoes Paul's encouragement in 2 Corinthians 5:7. We live by faith, not by sight. If God were always visible — if I lived in a permanent state of trash-dump worship — then faith wouldn't be necessary. Commitment wouldn't be necessary either. It would be too easy.

On a summer day in Amarillo, you can hear the neighborhood ice cream truck for a long time before it finally arrives on your block. I'm not sure what ice cream trucks elsewhere do to announce their presence, but ours plays "Pop! Goes the Weasel" over its loudspeaker in an endless loop. *Endless.* I can't imagine how ice cream truck drivers deal with it on a daily basis.

When the first notes of the song begin, blocks away, you know the truck is in the neighborhood. But you can't see it, and you're never sure when you should stop your game of soccer in the yard and run to the curb. So you wait. And wait. Finally the truck turns the corner, and that faint melody becomes so loud you can't hear anything else.

Faith is like that. It's believing that God will arrive, even if you can barely hear his song right now. Faith is not what you have when God is parked in front of your house. My faith doesn't rest on Philippians 2:5, and it's not sustained by a sweaty concert in Managua. Faith is hardly needed during those God-is-real experiences. I need faith during all the other times. I need faith when I'm streamside, waiting for Dad, imagining what's gone wrong.

Has my faith remained strongest — out of necessity — during the dry years? In the valleys between the mountaintops and the deserts between the gardens? Is faith simply what remains when God is absent?

chapter 5

Reverse Bricklaying

There's a joke about a journalist who was working in Jerusalem. The journalist heard about an elderly Jewish man who had been making a trip to the Wailing Wall to pray, twice a day, for many years. She thought he might make for a good feature, so she went to the wall, hoping to interview the man.

It didn't take long. Using a cane, the old man shuffled up to the wall. The journalist watched him pray, vigorously, for the next forty-five minutes. When he finished, she approached him.

"If you don't mind me asking, sir, how long have you been coming to the Wailing Wall to pray?"

"For sixty years," he answered.

"Sixty years! That's amazing. What do you pray for?"

"In the morning, I pray for peace between the Christians, Jews, and Muslims. I pray that there will be peace between Israel and Palestine. Then, in the afternoon, I pray for the wars and hatred to stop and that there will be peace between all men. I pray that our children will grow up in safety."

"And, if I may ask, how do you feel after doing this for so many years?"

The old man looked at her and shrugged. "Like I'm talking to a brick wall."

My biggest sin is prayerlessness. As far as sins go, I'm in ancient company. In the Old Testament, the prophet Samuel told the Israelites, "Far be it from me that I should sin against the Lord by failing to pray for you" (1 Samuel 12:23). Jesus told his disciples the parable about the persistent widow "to show them that they should always pray and not give up" (Luke 18:1). Paul instructed the members of the church at Thessalonica to "pray continually" (1 Thessalonians 5:17). But despite those few passages, lack of prayer gets very little attention — biblically or otherwise. It misses out on the "thou shalt not" treatment in the Ten Commandments. It doesn't show up on any contemporary lists of Top Sins, either, which tend to favor trendy new sins like voting for Democrats or supporting gay marriage.

But Jesus thought highly of prayer. He taught his disciples by example, thanks to his habit of going off by himself to pray early in the morning. He also taught them to pray by saying things like, "This, then, is how you should pray . . ." (Matthew 6:9 – 13 and also Luke 11:2 – 4), which is fairly straightforward for someone so enamored with parables and metaphors.

But I don't pray. Not enough. I suspect my lack of prayer contributes to my doubt and unbelief. Prayer, after all, is an admission that I need God—that I can't get by without him. If God seems distant to me, maybe it's because my self-reliance amplifies that feeling.

Would my faith be stronger if I spoke to God more often? If so, then why don't I pray? I have my reasons.

Some of them are theological. The idea of God's sovereign rule over the universe—that God is aware of and in control over everything that ever happens—is a standard (albeit profound) belief among most Christians. That being the case, I can't get past the one big question it leads to: Why must we ask for things when, according to Matthew 6:8, God is already aware of whatever we need? Do I think my prayers are actually informing God about bad things he should prevent, or blessings he ought to deliver, or situations he needs to resolve? If the puzzle is already assembled, at least from a heavenly perspective, why do we need to keep pointing out the pieces? Why does he need our help? Won't he do what he intends to do anyway?

Not only does God already know my needs, but he also knows what I might tell him in prayer. Should I pour my heart out to God about my doubts? Surely he knows they exist. Confess my sins? The Bible commands me to do so, but it also says God is perfectly aware of my sins already. Use him as a sounding board? Tell him what I'm feeling? Honestly, I prefer my wife's feedback on that stuff. She gives clearer opinions.

That's a little glib, I know, but the questions are serious, and I'm not the first person to ask them. Having grown up in church, I'm aware of the primary reason why we *should* pray: We pray, not to change God's mind, but to change ourselves. Prayer is a way of aligning our will with the will of God: "Your kingdom come, your will be done." That's a perfectly fine argument, but it's an argument *we* make in trying to justify the convoluted theology of prayer. Because the Bible's teachings on prayer are not at all clear.

Taken alone, James 4:2 is a great justification for prayer: "You do not have because you do not ask God." But in his well-known "consider the lilies of the field" passage, Jesus takes a different approach. He says that the Father not only knows what we need but will provide it for us—whether we ask or not (Matthew 7:25–34). Then in Romans 8:25-27, Paul writes that the Holy Spirit intercedes on our behalf when we don't know how to pray—and he does so in accordance with God's will.

So which is it? I need faith, and I have asked God to increase my faith. Presumably, God wants me to *have* increased faith. Even if I didn't realize it, the Spirit has probably been asking God—however that works—to improve my faith. So why am I still so faith-challenged?

I don't get it, and the biblical writers aren't helping. Our prayer life is informed by our understanding of God, and this is one thing I don't understand. My prayer life suffers from that lack of understanding.

It's not just the theology of prayer that gives me hangups. I am also defeated by my attempts to practice it. I would guess that, for most Christians, the majority of prayers are prayed silently. Yet I am virtually incapable of silent prayer. The practice of praying in my head—of lining up stray thoughts to present them to God in an official, well-reasoned, and coherent manner—is like sweeping marbles with a push-broom on a gym floor. I can't sustain it for any length of time before everything scatters. Praying aloud is a minor help, because psychologically it feels much more like a person-to-person conversation. But the opportunities to do this without looking like a mental patient are rare. Sometimes I pray audibly when I'm alone in my car, but I feel weird about it. I've considered wearing a fake Bluetooth earpiece so other drivers will think I'm on the phone.

And even if praying aloud in private may be a solution to Scattered Thoughts Syndrome, I hate praying aloud in public too—whether it's me praying or someone else. Despite how hard I try, it's very difficult for me to pray in front of people without slipping into self-absorption. I start wondering how I sound and what my "audience" thinks of my prayer. *Are they impressed by those biblical allusions? Are they intrigued by this glimpse into my interior spiritual life? Look how I worked in that obscure Old Testament messianic reference!* I never feel more like a Pharisee, doing religious stuff to get attention, than when I pray in public.

And I never become more judgmental than when I listen to other people pray in public. At the risk of sounding like a crotchety old geezer, I have an unimaginably low tolerance for the annoying clichés of spontaneous public prayer. These include the following: using a breathy prayer voice that's totally different from your normal way of speaking; peppering every verb with the fake-humble qualifier word "just"; using the words "God" and "Lord" and "Father" in place of commas, as if you need to keep reminding God we're talking to him; and reminding God of things that are in the Bible as a way to inject a little sermonizing into public prayer. The reason I keep my eyes closed when other people pray is so no one sees me rolling them.

So to say I'm conflicted about prayer is an understatement. I'm disillusioned and bitter about prayer — as if that fact isn't clear from the paragraph above — and part of my problem has to do with the half-encounter with God I mentioned in the last chapter.

There was a time in my life when I desperately wanted to be a charismatic, Pentecostal, drenched-in-the-Holy-Spirit Christian. I went to Brazil on a church mission trip the summer after my freshman year in college. I was nineteen, in the middle of falling in love with my future wife, and still figuring out that whole humility thing from my encounter with God on the yellow couch in my basement.

It was a partnership missions trip, which is a Southern Baptist concept in which churchgoers from the United States spend several days working with local churches in another country. These trips were primarily evangelistic, involving full days of door-to-door "witnessing," during which we explained to people the plan of salvation (sin leads to separation from God, which can only be repaired by Christ's death on the cross), attempted to lead them in saying the Sinner's Prayer, and invited them to church services that night.

Every morning our team would head out to share the gospel with random people on the streets and in the neighborhoods of these churches. Every evening we'd come back to our hotel after the church services, and we'd rejoice in the numbers of people who were saved. Yes, we kept count: numbers were a big deal. We all had stories about "leading people to the Lord," and we told these stories to each other in detail.

It began to occur to me on this trip that quite a few of those we convinced to say the Sinner's Prayer along with us were Catholic Christians who already believed in, worshiped, and loved Jesus — only they didn't describe their faith in him using the words and formulas we wanted them to use.[1] So when we asked whether they'd invited Jesus into their hearts, they'd say no, because Catholics don't talk that way.

But we were aggressive, persuasive Americans. And Catholics like to recite prayers. So when we asked them to follow us as we led them in praying the prayer of salvation, they almost always agreed to it. The result? We got to see "many souls saved." Only it was becoming clear to me that an embarrassing number of those saved souls were (1) probably saved already, just not in the way we Baptists preferred to talk about it; or (2) trying to make us Americans happy, and if an American wants you to pray with them, it's polite to do so;[2] or (3) trying to get us to go away.

If anyone else felt the same way I did, we didn't talk about it much. These mission trips were such a big deal

---

1. Brazil is said to be the largest Roman Catholic country in the world, with more than three-quarters of its population declaring Roman Catholicism as their religion.

2. This was the early 1990s, when people in other countries were immediately impressed with you simply because you were an American. These days, things are a bit different.

at our church. My mom had been to Brazil when I was a kid. My future mother-in-law went multiple times and always came back with these amazing stories. My friends and classmates were there with me, and they seemed just as excited about the decisions and stories and evangelism opportunities.

But not me. This was around the time I'd begun reading a broader selection of Christian writers, including Catholics like Henri Nouwen and Brennan Manning. My religious outlook was in the process of expanding. I couldn't see myself trying to get Henri Nouwen to ask Jesus into his heart. These poor Brazilians weren't as educated and insightful as Nouwen, of course, but that didn't make the evangelism feel less icky to me. Recently, grace had opened the windows to my faith, but this mission trip was turning me into a cynic.

By the week's end, I was burned out and annoyed and doubting the usefulness of the whole enterprise. I was ready to go home. A few days before we returned to the States, though, a college guy named Mark stumbled upon our group. Mark was from Oklahoma and was concluding a three-month stay in Brazil as a summer missionary. Mark and I had a lot in common. He was skeptical about the evangelism stuff too, because what he'd found in Brazil was way more exciting than going around telling Catholics about Jesus.

Mark, another born-and-bred Baptist kid, had discovered the Holy Spirit. Not in the safe Southern Baptist way, but in the wild and wonder-filled Pentecostal way.

He told me about traveling to hear an old British missionary speak in São Paulo. According to Mark's recap, the missionary had a white goatee and some convincing stories about the Holy Spirit's dramatic activities in Brazil. After the talk was over, the old man invited his audience down to the front of the church to be "baptized with the Holy Spirit."[3] Mark heeded the invitation, gathered at the altar with everyone else, held out his hands palms-up in a receptive gesture (as directed by the speaker), and repeated a prayer to ask God to fill him with the Holy Spirit.

According to Mark, what happened next felt like electricity surging through him, evidenced by the fact that his hands clenched up involuntarily. The missionary told those at the front to start praying aloud — in expectation that the gift of tongues would arrive along with the Holy Spirit, just like had happened in Acts 2. Mark reported that his prayer was in regular English (he was disappointed), but some of the people around him began speaking in tongues. Nevertheless, my new friend was certain he'd received what the

---

3. Definition: an experience of Pentecostals and charismatic Christians, usually occurring after salvation, during which the Holy Spirit "fills" you and quite possibly gives you special powers like speaking in tongues or prophecy — or dancing during worship songs.

missionary called the "Second Blessing," and he was praying that eventually God would give him some good old-fashioned glossolalia as proof of that Holy Spirit baptism.

This was new stuff to me. Even though my reading list had expanded to include Episcopalians and Catholics, I was still a Southern Baptist kid who'd been taught that charismatic Christians were just like the crazy televangelists I'd seen on TV. They were deluded, theologically wrong, and . . . well, *weird*. But Mark was normal. And passionate. We had a lot of discussions about faith during those few days in Brazil, and by the last day of our trip, he had convinced me that I needed to be baptized by the Holy Spirit too. The contemporary evangelical church, he told me, had totally lost sight of the Holy Spirit's power. To see what we were missing, all you had to do was read the book of Acts, which had lots of miraculous healings and demon encounters and powerful Spirit stuff.

I agreed. As a teenager struggling with spiritual problems like doubt and disillusionment, I was open to a better version of Christianity. I wanted what Mark had, and I was willing to try anything. So in our hotel, a few hours before our return flight, Mark prayed for me. He instructed me to hold my hands in a receptive position, like he had. I closed my eyes. Facing me, he put one hand on my shoulder and one hand in the air and started praying with a tone of voice that, depending on your perspective, was either very confident or very demanding. He commanded the Holy Spirit to come down and fill me. He repeated it over and over, and at one point put his hand on my chest and pushed against me. I didn't feel any electricity, but my heart started racing because it was an intense experience.

A couple of minutes into the prayer, I opened my eyes and saw that my hands were clenched. Finally, concluding the prayer, Mark said, "Now, praise him out loud. Cry out to God!"

I hesitated.

"Do it!" he said. "Pray!"

I mumbled, "Thank you, Jesus," a couple of times, knowing this was the part where the speaking in tongues was supposed to start, and wondering how it would happen and what it might feel like. But nothing happened.

(Confession: At this point in life, I had spent very little time among charismatics and didn't really even know what "speaking in tongues" sounded like. Had I been more experienced, I probably could have faked it. In fact, I probably *would* have faked it.)

The whole moment was very dramatic and exciting. The fact that my hands were clenched up at the end — just like Mark's hands had clenched! — really surprised me. Maybe, I hoped, that physical response was a manifestation of a spiritual reality. I had the distinct impression that something sacred and strange had happened. Mark had prayed and spoken with such authority. Such conviction. Whatever had happened, it was new and it was powerful.

I figured I had just been baptized by the Holy Spirit.

When I returned home, I tried to act, at least in certain churchy situations, like the newly charismatic Christian I had supposedly become. Unlike the Philippians "conversion," which propelled me in the direction of humility and service, this one launched me into spiritual confidence. I was convinced I had taken my first steps along the path toward becoming a Spirit-filled believer. And based on Mark's experiences and example—a good three or four days of it—I knew exactly what that looked like. It looked like authority. Like boldness before God. Like intense conviction. In other words, it revolutionized my prayer life.

I only told a couple of people about what had happened in Brazil (one of them was my girlfriend/wife-to-be). But I'm pretty sure more than a couple noticed that my prayers at church or in home Bible studies had suddenly become a lot more daring. Both publicly and privately, my prayers shifted toward the dramatic. My vocal inflection became very, very serious. I began claiming promises from the Bible and insisting that God hold fast to them. I started ordering the Holy Spirit around. I added some spiritual warfare to my prayer life — that's what charismatics did, after all — identifying demonic spirits and rebuking the Devil and throwing the name of Jesus at them like a verbal talisman. I devoured books about prayer and the Holy Spirit and speaking in tongues by authors like Jack Hayford and Dick Eastman.

Over and over again, with genuine passion, I pleaded with God to bless me with the gift of tongues. I begged for it. I mustered up as much faith as I could. I claimed the "strong name of Jesus" (I'd heard others do this). I wanted that gift more than just about anything. It would be proof, after all, that my second blessing was authentic, that it wasn't just some psychological neediness that resulted in hand-clenching. Proof that something really had happened in Brazil.

This period — my season of audacious prayer and theatrical faith — lasted about a year. And guess what?

Nothing happened. I never prayed in tongues. My newfound spiritual enthusiasm devolved into performance art, as my focus devolved from a passion for God (which was authentic) into concern about what people thought of the newly authoritative and spiritually profound Jason. Did they see me as a powerful, different kind of Christian? Were they transfixed by my bold prayers? What did they think about my insight into the spiritual world? Did it inspire them? Shock them? Scare them a little?

If so, good. I'd become convinced we Baptist kids were totally missing out on real faith, real Christianity, the real Holy Spirit. Wanna see it for real? Check *me* out.

I had become, once again, a self-involved jerk. This lasted until a few months before my wedding, when the spiritual doubt gradually seeped back in. Remembering my earlier quest for humility, I finally saw myself for who I'd become. I realized that whatever happened in Brazil had not turned me into a super-spiritual, super-power-ful, super-godly follower of Jesus. On the contrary, it had turned me into a super-arrogant showman. Regardless of what you think the Holy Spirit does in the believer's life, it's probably not that.

Upon recognizing this, I abandoned my charismatic pursuit as quickly as I'd taken it up and pretty much soured on the whole drama. I still have never spoken in tongues. And looking back now, I wonder if anything really *did* happen in Brazil. Did my hands clench up because God did something physical to me? That's what I wanted to believe. But you know what else occurs to me? I was standing with my hands in an uncomfortable position for several minutes. And I knew that clenched hands had been, for Mark, a "proof" of God's power. Maybe I clenched my hands subconsciously. Did I feel something "electric" because the Spirit was moving? Or because I *expected* to feel something?

Did anything genuinely supernatural happen? I don't know. I really don't. What I *do* know is that the experience made me a worse person. I'm pretty sure that's *not* the desired outcome of a legitimate encounter with the Holy Spirit.

At any rate, I learned one thing from my wannabe-charismatic adventure: Never before had I prayed so passionately, so regularly, and so fervently as I had during those months. I prayed for people to be healed. I prayed for unsuspecting friends to be delivered from spiritual oppression. I prayed for my church to open up to the power of the Spirit. I prayed for the ability to speak in tongues.

Not one of those prayers seems to have been answered. Not even close. Despite the drama, it felt like I was praying to a brick wall. It still feels that way. My prayer life has been pretty sorry ever since.

If there is a wall between me and God, of course, it's one I've built myself. I've laid bricks of apathy that reflect my questions about whether prayer is worth the time. Bricks of confusion as I've struggled with prayers that treat God less like our creator and more like my concierge. Bricks of sin that, because of guilt or shame or personal disappointment, dampen my desire to be in God's presence. Bricks of cynicism when I can't say my own public prayer or listen to another's without hearing a fake monologue addressed to

God but aimed at everyone else. Bricks of doubt and disbelief that make me question whether there's even a God who hears my prayer.

You can build an imposing wall with that many bricks. I've been praying to that wall so long that I hardly want to pray anymore.

But I still pray. I make myself do it for one simple reason: Jesus prayed. He seemed to think it a worthy pursuit, and he taught his disciples to pray too. If I'm supposed to be following his teachings — which is always a good goal for Christians — then I need to pray. One of the things that makes Christianity unique is its promise of a personal relationship with God. Even if I don't understand the theology of it, it seems obvious that honest, vulnerable communication — which is what prayer is, at least from my end — can only deepen that relationship. If I've built a wall between me and God, then prayer is as good a way as any to knock it down.

I've come to see prayer as the art of tearing down that wall, brick by brick. It's hard work. How in the world do you begin to pray when you don't understand prayer, barely tolerate prayer, and can't find the discipline to get beyond your prayer hang-ups?

The answer surprised me, and it will probably surprise a lot of other Baptists and other low-church evangelical types. But really, it's pretty simple: Liturgy taught me to pray again.

Thomas Merton writes that the best way to progress in prayer is to pray in a way that makes you experience your own nothingness and poverty. The best prayers take our focus off ourselves.[4] That's what liturgical prayer does for me. In praying with others' words instead of my own, I'm freed up from concerns about sentence structure and dramatic phrasing and whether or not anyone's impressed with my word choice. It frees me up from worrying about expressing enough emotion or authority or faith. As I once heard Don Golden say, "A liturgy is something we put on our lips when we don't feel it in our hearts."[5]

Amen. Liturgical prayer is how I pray when I don't feel much like praying. Which is most of the time.

Using scripted prayers was uncomfortable at first. It felt inauthentic. Then again, I come from a religious culture that values personal, spontaneous prayer and suspects liturgical prayer as being the empty words and "vain repetition" Jesus warned about in Matthew 6:7. Those who employ that verse as an anti-liturgical weapon generally point it at

4. Blogger Alan Creech (alancreech.com) turned me on to this Merton statement, which I'm paraphrasing. It's from a collection of Merton's letters called *The Hidden Ground of Love* (New York: Harcourt, 1993).

5. Golden, who co-authored *Jesus Wants to Save Christians* with Rob Bell, said this in a sermon he gave at Mars Hill Bible Church in Grandville, Michigan.

Catholics and other high-church traditions, forgetting that contemporary evangelicals use a lot of empty words of their own. *(We just come to you right now, Father God, in the name of Jesus, asking you to fill us so our words won't be empty, Lord God, so we won't sound like Pharisees but will be totally real with you, Jesus.)*

Earlier in that Matthew 6 passage, Jesus mentions people who "love to pray standing in the synagogues and on the street corners to be seen by others" (v. 5). He calls them hypocrites. I can relate. Been there, done that.

I don't pray much in public anymore. If I do, I try to go heavy on the gratitude and light on the requests. And when I pray in private, rarely are my words my own. Instead, I borrow from the deep traditions of Christianity. I'll use prayers from the Bible, of course, along with scripture-based prayers from the Eastern Orthodox tradition, prayers from the church fathers, and selections from the *Book of Common Prayer.*

How are these better than the spontaneous prayers I stammer out at church? Let me count the ways. These prayers are biblically rich, theologically deep, and lyrically beautiful. But that's not what gives them meaning. What moves me is the fact that devout Christians have been praying these words for centuries. By joining them, I'm stepping into the same stream of faith as the early Christians, the martyrs and the saints, the medieval monks and common-language translators, the Reformers and Puritans and nineteenth-century revivalists.

If given the choice between resting in the prayers they prayed, or trusting myself to come up with something better off the top of my head, I'm siding with the ancients.

So I regularly find myself praying the same Lord's Prayer I learned in seventh-grade basketball. It's hard to improve on a prayer found in the Bible and taught by Jesus, though you wouldn't know it, based on the number of times I've ever said the Lord's Prayer in a Baptist church. Which is maybe twice. (And one of those times, I led it.)

Often, my prayers are confessional. The short, simple "Jesus Prayer" is my favorite. It's an ancient prayer from Eastern Orthodox Christianity, adapted from the humble tax collector's plea in Jesus' parable (Luke 18:9 – 14). I mumble this prayer as often as I think of it during the day: *Lord Jesus Christ, son of the living God, have mercy on me, a sinner.*

That short sentence covers a lot of bases. It acknowledges Jesus as Lord, which Paul says is at the heart of the Christian faith (see Romans 10:9). Asking for mercy and confessing my sinfulness puts me in a position of humility. This seems an appropriate posture for a doubter like me. Though the theology of prayer doesn't always make sense, asking for mercy certainly does. I could pray that every minute of the day, and it still would be heartfelt.

More formally, I find myself increasingly drawn to the "Confession of Sin" from the Anglican *Book of Common Prayer,* which I've grown to love over the last few years:

Most merciful God,
>*we confess that we have sinned against you*
>*in thought, word, and deed,*
>*by what we have done,*
>*and by what we have left undone.*

We have not loved you with our whole heart;
>*we have not loved our neighbors as ourselves.*

We are truly sorry and we humbly repent.

For the sake of your Son Jesus Christ,
>*have mercy on us and forgive us;*
>*that we may delight in your will,*
>*and walk in your ways,*
>*to the glory of your Name. Amen.*[6]

If you get a chance to pray this among a community of believers, it's a very powerful thing. The opportunities

---

6. This is from "The Holy Eucharist: Rite Two" in the 1979 version of the *Book of Common Prayer,* which you can find at www.bcponline.org and hear in an Episcopal church near you. Also, it's on page 360 of my little red BCP: *Book of Common Prayer and Administration of the Sacraments and Other Rites and Ceremonies of the Church* (New York: Oxford University Press, 1990).

for me to pray this in church are rare, so I make it singular instead of plural: *I am truly sorry and I humbly repent . . .* I'm hoping the Episcopalians will forgive me.

I've altered and combined a few other prayers from the *Book of Common Prayer* that I pray individually for my wife and two children. The best prayers on their behalf, though, are the simple and authentic ones, like *Help me.* People tend to reserve that one for emergencies, but I think it works best when used frequently. As a husband, as a father — even as a writer — it's almost always appropriate. *Thank You* is another all-purpose prayer. I learned it from my parents, who taught me how important it was to say *thank you* as often as possible. Show gratitude to grown-ups. To friends. To God. I'm trying to teach my kids the same thing.

So I'm learning to pray again, and I'm learning to pray for what seem to be the right reasons. Other than requests for grace and forgiveness and my daily bread, I hardly ask for anything anymore — especially not for myself, and *especially* not for the gift of tongues. I pray for my family. I do a lot of confessing, because I have not loved God with my whole heart or my neighbors as myself. I try to say thanks a lot too, because gratitude is a good weapon against doubt. It's hard to doubt God's existence when I keep thanking him for stuff.

But mostly I pray because Jesus prayed. He taught his

disciples to pray, and I guess he's teaching me, too. I still have to put in the effort, of course, when it comes to removing the wall, brick by brick. But the tools are not my own. They come from somewhere else — from deep traditions, from ancient communities of faith, from classic spiritual writings, from the Son of the living God.

Rather than diminish my spiritual life, praying with others' words actually *increases* my faith. It gives me something to pray when I can't generate the words myself. It teaches me humility and graciousness. It shows me that prayer is less about the attitude than the action. Praying ancient words of confession brings me to a place of repentance. Praying ancient words of gratitude somehow expands my Grinch-like heart. With liturgy, I pray my way into true prayer.

chapter 6

Insanity at 900 Feet

As a kid, I used to tell people that roller coasters made me throw up, but that was a lie. Motion sickness is a weird thing to lie about, but to me it seemed preferable to telling the truth: I was scared of big roller coasters. Soil-my-britches scared.

My fear was based only on conjecture, because until eighth grade I'd never even been on a real roller coaster. I got over that fear when I rode the Shock Wave for the first time at Six Flags over Texas. I don't remember the specifics of my decision to trust my life to the laws of physics and a tiny little lap bar, but I'd wager a girl was involved.

That day, I discovered that I really, really like thrill rides.

I've been trying to make up for my years of thrill abstinence ever since, subjecting myself to as many roller coasters and freefall rides as possible. And despite my childhood fears, it's rare that a roller coaster actually scares me. Sure, the height makes me nervous. The combination of adrenaline and anticipation gives me a nice little natural buzz. But only one thrill ride has filled me with genuine fear, to the point where I'm not sure I would ride it again if given the chance.

That ride is called Insanity, and you can find it on the Las Vegas Strip at the top of the Stratosphere tower and casino. The Stratosphere is 1,149 feet tall, which makes it the tallest freestanding tower in the United States and the second-tallest observation tower in the Western Hemisphere. Its observation deck, at nearly 900 feet, is surpassed in height only by a few skyscrapers. Above this observation deck are three rides — the three highest thrill rides in the world.

Two of them aren't much to write home about. But Insanity, the third one, lives up to its name. At the top of the Stratosphere, riders sit in seats attached to a huge mechanical arm that swings more than sixty feet out over the edge of the tower — with nothing but the Strip 900 feet below — and begins to spin the riders around. As you spin faster and faster, the centrifugal force tilts the ride's seats outward until you hit a seventy-degree angle, which is pretty much face down. If you summon up the courage to keep your eyes open, you'll look straight down and see nothing but concrete and ant-sized gamblers ninety stories below.

I nearly wet my pants just standing in line.

What makes Insanity so gut-churningly intense, of course, is its location at the top of the Stratosphere. The actual movement of the ride — the high-speed, face-down spinning part — is plenty of fun, but it's no different from the centrifugal-force rides you can find at your favorite amusement park. But attach that movement to a tower high above Las Vegas, and you get one of the best thrill rides in the world. The terror comes not from *what* the ride does, but from *where* it does it: 900 feet up in the air.

Context makes it scary. Context gives it power.

What I'm learning about doubt — and specifically about the causes of doubt — is that context is everything. Context plays a huge role in how much we allow our doubts to annoy, worry, frighten, or paralyze us. The further removed we get from these doubt-generators, the less power they have, and the less we allow them to hijack our faith.

What causes doubt or spiritual uncertainty? One major factor is sin. A crucial Christian doctrine is the idea that sin separates us from God. Here's how the process usually works: You sin. Maybe you have a long history of habitual sins, like an addiction to pornography or a lifetime of flexibility with the truth. Or perhaps a bunch of increasingly serious sins — selfishness, lust, dishonesty — finally culminate in a moral failure like adultery. Whatever the case, sin usually produces guilt. In the best cases, that guilt leads to repentance.

But not always. Sometimes guilt results in a feeling of isolation and distance. God seems far away. Forgiveness sounds nice in theory, but it hardly seems appropriate given the depths of your failure. Grace? A pipe dream. We explain this feeling of separation and distance from God by telling ourselves that God is holy; he can't abide sin. Since we are scum, God can't be around us. So we never take that next step toward restoration. We refuse grace. Angry or hurt or ashamed, we choose to embrace the martyrdom of being shut off from God.

The longer we live in that guilty isolation, the further away God feels. Finally, we're so far removed from him — it's been *so* long — we lose any spiritual awareness we once had. Prayer feels fake. Religion seems empty. The whole sandwich gets spoiled. And when something goes really bad, you don't scrape off the mold so you can find the good parts. You just throw the whole thing away.

We see this in the poetry of King David of Israel, who bedded his next-door neighbor Bathsheba and had her husband killed. This catastrophic chain of sin pounded the doubt into his thoughts, which found expression in many of his psalms. He continually asks for restoration, calling for God to remain near and longing for God to come out of hiding. "Do not cast me from your presence," he writes, "or take your Holy Spirit from me " (Psalm 51:11).

David wasn't alone in struggling with sin-related

doubt. Though sinless, Jesus also dealt with doubt—and with its spiritual isolation—during the crucifixion. He suffered for hours on the cross, having personally taken on the sins of the world, then cried out at the end, "My God, my God, why have you forsaken me?" He's quoting David here, who asked the same question in Psalm 22:1, finishing the thought with "Why are you so far from saving me?"[1] Jesus knew how sin could distance a person from God. He experienced it firsthand.

Another doubt-producer, oddly enough, is familiarity. Have you ever looked at a common word like "pumpkin" or "vacuum" and thought, *That's the goofiest word I've ever seen. Is that really how it's spelled?* Sometimes I look at Christianity that way.

Familiarity can breed contempt—or boredom. Don't get me wrong: I love the church, despite her flaws and shallowness and child abuse scandals. In a world that needs grace, there is no better poster girl for grace than the church. But the more the gatherings of Christians turn into an institution—with fundraising campaigns, endless programming, and boards of elders and committees and deacons—the more the crazy revolutionary teachings of Jesus

1. Jesus' question is in Matthew 27:46 and Mark 15:34. A few theologians and historians have wondered whether the gospel writers purposefully connected this question to a well-known psalm in order to soften a moment of doubt they thought was inappropriate for the Messiah.

become oatmeal. Watery, tasteless oatmeal. And I get tired of oatmeal pretty fast.

The great Polish-born piano virtuoso Arthur Rubinstein was once asked if he believed in God. "No. I don't believe in God," Rubinstein said. "I believe in something greater."[2]

My American evangelical Christian religion doesn't always allow God to be great, and occasionally the less-than-great God is the one I doubt. He's the deity who always backs a certain political party, or a particular social issue, or who never fails to side with us. He's the God who always smiles proudly upon the dedications of our multimillion-dollar church buildings and rejoices when a teenager gets "saved" for the third time. He's the God who showers us with financial blessings but never with poverty, who rewards us with business success but never with failure, who's totally cool with the money we spend on concert lighting in the worship center while the widow down the block has a hole in her roof.

I don't believe in that God. If I'm going to draw close to God, it needs to be a God who's greater than that.

For many people, depression is a root cause of doubt. Some of us struggle to trust God when things are great.

---

2. I first heard this story from an essay by Umberto Eco, "God Isn't Big Enough for Some People," in Britain's *The Daily Telegraph* (November 27, 2005).

When things fall apart, it's even harder. Especially in a culture that tends to see every good thing — a new job, a high-paying career, a sweet parking spot — as a blessing from God. This is an idea we've carried over from Old Testament culture, where success (in the form of abundant livestock or a productive harvest) was often viewed as a direct blessing from God.

But in the New Testament, Jesus turns this idea on its head. In Matthew 5:45, he says God sends his rain on the righteous and the unrighteous alike. Earlier in that chapter, in the famous Beatitudes, he says that those who mourn are blessed — along with the meek, the persecuted, and the poor in spirit (Matthew 5:3 – 10). None of these sound like worldly success.[3] But if we're convinced that success of any kind comes from God, rightly or wrongly, then a lack of success is bound to cause us to question God.

David did this all the time.

How long, Lord? Will you forget me forever?
How long will you hide your face from me?
How long must I wrestle with my thoughts
and day after day have sorrow in my heart?
    (Psalm 13:1 – 2)

---

3. The belief that financial rewards and the things our culture views as "success" should automatically be attributed to God is usually called the Prosperity Gospel, but it's not the gospel at all.

That's some pretty serious doubt, and I even cut the quote before David starts contemplating death. The transition from "How long, Lord?" to "Are you even there, God?" to, eventually, "Oh, forget it" is a fairly easy one, especially in the face of senseless tragedy or heartache. When life fails you, and you end up with a daily allowance of sorrow in your heart, doubt is a natural choice.

The great Old Testament prophet Elijah made that choice. Despite being praised by New Testament writers as a man of great faith, Elijah got depressed after the wicked queen Jezebel had threatened him with death. He took off into the wilderness of Horeb, where he sat down under a tree and wallowed in his misfortune. Before long, he was asking God to kill him.[4] And why not? His life seemed utterly hopeless.

Right: *Hopeless.* Keep in mind that this is a guy who had personally brought a widow's dead son back to life and who recently had called down fire from heaven in a spiritual showdown with the prophets of Baal, making them look like a bunch of deluded numbskulls who had run out of magic tricks. All that power and drama. All those legitimate visual displays of God's presence. Then Elijah gets depressed, and suddenly he turns into a doubter.

---

4. "I have had enough, Lord," he said. "Take my life" (1 Kings 19:4).

Crazy? Maybe a little. You pretty much *had* to be crazy to be an Old Testament prophet. But just as it's easy to trust God's provision when you're being fed by ravens, as Elijah was, it's also easy to doubt God's goodness when life doesn't seem so good anymore.

What about circumstances? They can lead to doubt too, as the Elijah story makes very clear. Or consider the story of John the Baptist, a guy who had pretty good reason to maintain faith in Jesus. He was there, after all, when Jesus kicked off his adult ministry by being baptized in the Jordan River — an event punctuated by no less than the audible voice of God.

And yet, after having been arrested by Herod Antipas, John the Baptist started wondering about the whole thing. Was Jesus really who he said he was? From jail, John dispatched his own disciples to ask a doubt-drenched question of Jesus: "Are you the one who was to come, or should we expect someone else?" (Matthew 11:3).

Jesus pointed John to the evidence that he was, indeed, the Messiah. But don't let that gloss over the fact that a prophetic, holy, God-infused person like John the Baptist — someone who had touched Jesus, who knew him better than most, who saw the miracles from the front row — still struggled with faith when his life didn't turn out the way he expected.

Circumstances can draw us to God, but they can also

pull us away from him. Ask any widow or widower. Ask anyone devastated by tragedy.

Or ask the disciples, because John the Baptizer wasn't alone in his hesitation. Matthew 28 reports that after Jesus' death and burial the remaining eleven disciples (without Judas) had gathered in Galilee to meet Jesus. They'd been instructed to do so by the women who first encountered the risen Christ near the empty tomb. So when Jesus showed up among the disciples, the gospel account says, "they worshiped him; but some doubted" (v. 17).

Wait. Some *doubted*? These were guys who had lived with Jesus for three years. They too had observed and participated in the miracles. They'd heard him hint at his identity as the Messiah and the Son of God. They'd heard him predict his own death and resurrection. They knew what he smelled like, and they knew what made him laugh.

But then he died violently. Senselessly. He failed to live up to their expectations. So when Jesus showed up again — right there in the flesh, on a mountaintop — a few of them were able to look past their circumstances and remember what he'd taught. These disciples dropped to the ground in worship. But not all of them. Some doubted.

I'm not sure how to read this. Was it an either/or situation? A few disciples worshiped; others did not worship but doubted. Or was it both/and? The disciples worshiped. But some doubted *while* they worshiped. Either way, this is a fascinating response. Jesus was right there in front of them, resurrected, and so much more visible than a watercolor painting in a Bible or a stained-glass window in a sanctuary. But because their circumstances didn't match up with their expectations, they couldn't set aside their doubt.

But more than sin, familiarity, depression, and circumstances, we doubt because we're human. If you're afraid of doubt, being a human isn't your best option. We expend tons of energy trusting people and things we can see. When they let us down, who can blame us for struggling to trust Someone we can't see?[5] Doubting is part of our DNA.

In *The Heart of Christianity: Rediscovering a Life of Faith,* theologian Marcus Borg tells a story about a three-year-old girl who learned she was going to be a big sister. When her new brother came home from the hospital, the girl asked her parents if she could have some time alone with him — in his room, with the door shut. Her hesitant parents listened outside the door as their daughter leaned over the crib and whispered loudly to her baby brother.

"Tell me about God," the girl said to the newborn. "I've almost forgotten."[6]

Simply being alive, for many of us, is enough to sepa-

---

5. I expand on this in detail in chapter 8.

6. Marcus Borg, *The Heart of Christianity: Rediscovering a Life of Faith* (San Francisco: HarperOne, 2003), 114. Borg attributes this story to the Quaker scholar Parker Palmer.

rate us from God. Maybe we were close once, but the reality of living adds miles and miles to the distance. Some of us — and here I include myself, especially — have almost forgotten.

I've dealt with each of these doubt-generators at some point or another. We all have. What helps is realizing how big a role context plays in the intensity of our doubt. Other than the being human thing, these conditions are temporary. The doubts that seem so devastating and real in one season may eventually disappear. Context matters.

Despite his doubts in Psalm 13, David eventually came around. He leaned into God's unfailing love and rejoiced in his salvation (v. 5). Elijah encountered God during his depression, allowed God to take care of him, and then had his famous "still, small voice" experience (1 Kings 19 – 18). The disciples, who doubted the resurrected Jesus right there on the mountaintop, eventually took his message into Greece and Asia Minor and to the uttermost parts of the earth. Most of them were martyred for their faith. We don't know that their doubts disappeared, but we do know that they learned to move past them — or at least to live with them.

Most doubts come and go, intensified by the details of our lives. Like a thrill ride high above the ground, the intensity of these doubts is determined by our surroundings.

Separate the ride from its context, and there's less reason to be afraid.

Most of my doubts can best be handled with similar detachment. I let patience and time put some distance between me and whatever circumstances gave birth to the doubt. I wait until I learn to trust again. I wait until the simple actions of faith transform into real faith. That's all the valleys of doubt are — waiting.

But there's one cause of doubt that distance won't cure — and for many of us, it's the most problematic. It's a kind of doubt that isn't tied to our emotions or to something vague like "being human." It's intellectual doubt, and it's the hardest kind to shake. Galileo blamed God for this. "I do not feel obliged," the astronomer once said, "to believe that the same God who has endowed us with sense, reason, and intellect has intended us to forego their use."[7]

Bless you, Galileo. I'm no legendary Italian scientist, but I also seem to have a lot of trouble turning off the logical part of my brain. In the interest of honesty and full disclosure, I need to describe to you one of the big doubt generators I'm currently plugged into. Even as I write this chapter, I'm still feeling the effects of this most recent tumble into

7. Will and Ariel Durant, *The Age of Reason Begins: A History of European Civilization in the Period of Shakespeare, Bacon, Montaigne, Rembrandt, Galileo, and Descartes: 1558–1648* (New York: Simon & Schuster, 1961), 607.

doubt—this journey to a place where I'm actually allowing my mind to formulate questions like *Is this whole thing made up?*

And *Does God even exist?*

It happened while researching my most recent book, *Pocket Guide to the Afterlife*, which explores Christian beliefs about heaven and hell, along with the afterlife traditions of other world religions. Zoroastrianism really screwed me up.

If you are unfamiliar with history's back-of-the-alphabet religions, let me explain. Zoroastrianism is an ancient faith that stretches as far back as Judaism. Its founder, Zoroaster, was a nomadic tribesman and prophet in Persia, the part of the world we now know as Iran. Though some believe Zoroaster may have been a contemporary of Abraham, Zoroastrianism itself doesn't enter recorded history until 600 years prior to the birth of Christ.

As far as religions go, Zoroastrianism shares certain features with Judaism. It's monotheistic, with a supreme male deity named Ahura Mazda who created the universe.[8] Zoroaster's beliefs were also dualistic, in a soap-opera kind of way, because he taught that Ahura Mazda had an evil twin brother named Angra Manyu. While

---

8. Some scholars consider Zoroastrianism to be the world's first established monotheistic religion.

Ahura Mazda was the deity responsible for all the good in the world, Angra Manyu was to blame for the world's evil. The entirety of human history would reflect this conflict between the good god and the bad god until the whole thing ended in a violent apocalypse. The end of days would be preceded by a final judgment, at which time the faithful would be sent to paradise and the unfaithful would end up in a realm of punishment, where they'd be consumed by fire.

Yes, it sounds familiar. That's the problem.

Before we go any further, though, we need to talk about heaven and hell. These concepts are central to Christianity because they're all over the New Testament, especially the book of Revelation. But what many people don't realize is that much of the Old Testament doesn't really indicate that heaven and hell are our two possible destinations after death. In the Old Testament, the afterlife is hazy. The writers of the earliest Old Testament books—including Genesis, Exodus, Leviticus, Numbers, Deuteronomy, Job, Psalms, and Proverbs—clearly believed that, after death, people went to *sheol,* a shadowy netherworld thought to exist beneath the earth.[9] And everyone ended up there: the

---

9. *Sheol* appears sixty-five times in the Old Testament. In the King James Version, it was always translated as "hell." In more accurate modern versions, like the NIV, it's usually translated as "death" or "the grave," with a footnote that reads "Hebrew *Sheol*." See Psalm 49:14 for an example.

righteous and unrighteous, the just and the unjust, Levitical priests and pagan prostitutes.

On a related note, the Old Testament doesn't have a fully developed theology about the Devil, either. As an entity, he only appears a few times, and in all but one of these the original Hebrew doesn't call him by the personal name "Satan." Instead, it describes him as "the satan" (*hasatan*), as if it's a title. The most accurate translation of this title is "the accuser" or "the adversary." And he doesn't quite do what you'd expect. In Job, the *satan* appears to be a member of God's heavenly court and needs God's permission to test Job, like a prosecuting attorney under God's control. In Zechariah 3:1 – 7, the *satan* shows up again as part of God's council, voicing his opposition to the selection of Joshua, son of Jehozadak, as high priest.[10] In both passages, it seems to be the *satan*'s job to weed out lawbreakers or the unfaithful. But he has to do it with God's authorization. He is on God's team.

In 2 Samuel 24:1, God incites David to take a census of Israel. Weirdly, God causes David to do something that God actually condemns. So it's not surprising that in 1 Chronicles 21:1, a parallel account of the same story (but

---

10. 1 Kings 22:19 – 23 gives a good example of this idea of God having a "council." In this passage, the Almighty dispatches certain spirits to do his bidding — including "lying spirits" that entice prophets to lead people astray.

compiled by a different author), something has changed: it's not God who influences David, but Satan. This is the only place in the Old Testament where *Satan* is used as a proper name.

Nowhere in the Old Testament do we see the Devil, a personal and powerful deity who injects evil into the world, who sends demons out to tempt humans and persecute Christians, who rules a fiery hell, and who works against God while wearing a slimming red leotard. That stuff doesn't show up until the New Testament — and in the fourteenth-century literature of Dante.[11]

So what do *Satan* and *sheol* have to do with Zoroastrianism and my struggles with doubt?

In the parts of the Bible where God chooses Israel to be his people, sets them free from Egypt, explains to them the rules, gives them an incredibly detailed system of sin and repentance and sacrifice, and lays the groundwork for Judaism and eventually Christianity, God does *not* explain the central concepts of heaven and hell and the Devil. That stuff is absent from the Old Testament plot. But ask any Christian to detail the basics of his or her theology, and you'll get a heavy dose of heaven, hell, and Satan. These are big parts of the Christian worldview. And Jesus, the Son

---

11. Seriously. When it comes to popular depictions of hell and its tortures, we owe more to Dante's *Inferno* than to the Bible.

of God, talked about them. So if these theological ideas are not fully developed in the Old Testament, particularly the earliest parts, how did they suddenly end up in the New Testament?

The answer, according to many scholars, is that Jewish theology came into contact with Zoroastrianism. It likely happened during the Babylonian exile in the sixth century before Christ, because the Babylonians would have been Zoroastrians. It also could have happened around two hundred years before Jesus, during what's known as the Antiochian or Seleucid persecution of the Jews, because their oppressors during that time were also followers of Zoroaster. What we know is that, in the years between the writing of Malachi (at the end of the Old Testament) and the writing of the earliest gospels, a hell for sinners and an enemy of God called Satan—the proper name, not the title—began to show up in Jewish literature.[12] Before long, they cemented themselves in the Hebrew religion. Jesus taught them, Paul and Peter taught them, and they became central elements of the new Christian faith.

Do we Christians owe the ideas of Satan and hell to

---

12. A number of scholars date 1 Chronicles as having been written at least a century after 1 and 2 Samuel were written—and, conveniently, after the exile—which would explain how Satan ends up getting credit in 1 Chronicles 21:1 for an evil act that God orchestrates in 2 Samuel 24:1—because now there's someone better to blame.

Zoroastrianism? That's a big question on my mind these days.

The possible influence of Zoroastrianism on Judaism — and therefore on Christianity — fills me with uncertainty. It's obvious to me, as a student of world religions, that religious beliefs evolve over time. Christianity isn't immune to this, as the popularization of the Sinner's Prayer over the last century makes clear. It's a theological development that, in some circles, has taken on an important role in the Christian faith — and yet the earliest Christians probably wouldn't even recognize it. The fact that religions are influenced by human ideas is hardly a surprise, even when applied to our own faith. Change is inevitable.

But the existence of Satan and hell isn't just a cultural or theological shift. It's a major part of the Christian worldview. Much of that worldview derives from Judaism and has ancient roots, but hell and Satan just seem to show up out of nowhere in the couple of centuries before the time of Christ.

This fills me with questions: What does it mean when a central element of Christian theology seems to have come, not from God, but from a religion I think is pretty much false (Zoroastrianism)? If it wasn't borrowed from Zoroastrianism, then why did the theology of hell not appear until the New Testament? Aren't we supposed to believe that Satan and hell have been part of the story since creation—or at least since the so-called rebellion in heaven?[13] Then why does the evidence for this appear so haphazardly in the Bible?

Jesus treats the existence of hell as true, even though it's not clearly supported by the Old Testament—which Christians believe to be inspired Scripture and authoritative communication between God and his people. So what do we make of that? Did Satan and his fiery realm not emerge until right before Jesus came on the scene? If so, what's that about?

If I follow Jesus, and Jesus believes in hell and Satan, then do I also have to believe in hell and Satan? Even if the heroes of the faith—David and Moses and Joshua and Abraham—apparently had no idea about it? If a major reason for them to worship God and follow the Law was to avoid going to hell, why didn't God clue his people in about its existence? If I assume God didn't find Satan and his fiery realm important enough to explain to his chosen

---

13. A lot of conservative Christians equate the prophecy against the "king of Babylon" in Isaiah 14 and the "king of Tyre" in Ezekiel 28 as being symbolic retellings of the fall of the archangel Lucifer, in which he was cast out of heaven, along with his demons, at which point he became God's enemy. But just as many scholars believe this is a wishful interpretation of the text to bolster theology about Satan, when it's really just about, you know, the kings of Babylon and Tyre. I say "so-called" because the theology is disputed.

people, then why has it played such an important role in the two thousand years of Christianity?

One more question: Do I sound bitter because I spent much of my childhood afraid I was seconds away from an eternity of punishment in hell, when as an adult I'm discovering the biblical case for hell is not nearly as strong as I'd been taught?

Yes, I do sound bitter, because I am. Zoroastrianism and Satan are major stumbling blocks to my faith. It's not that there aren't reasonable answers to these questions, or even better questions than the ones I've just posed. I'm not a professional theologian or historian or biblical linguist. But I know enough to have serious questions about the religion I've practiced since childhood, and these questions are handcuffing my faith as an adult.

Anyway, I apologize for a heavy dose of historical and biblical detail — and for a lot of stuff that may have made you nervous, angry, or just plain bored. But I want you to understand that at least one of the reasons I struggle with doubt isn't sin or depression or unfavorable circumstances but roadblocks like education and logic. It's easy to apply Occam's Razor — remember from chapter 1? — to everything I've just described about Satan and hell and conclude that, well, the simplest answer is that the whole thing is all made up.

Maybe my religion is no more than a human mythology, assembled with parts from other cultures and beliefs over time. Which means it's not a major intellectual stretch to explain away God and the divinity of Jesus and the existence of heaven and hell as human constructs, no different from the stories about Zeus or Thor. Or Osiris. Or Mictlantecuhtli, the skeletal death god of Aztec theology who drips with blood and wears a necklace made out of human eyeballs.

Sigh. Now what?

chapter 7

This Is Horrible. Here, Taste It!

The last chapter ended with a tough question. You're probably waiting for the answer to it. What do you do when you encounter a serious intellectual challenge to your faith? Here are some options:

A. Read a Josh McDowell or Lee Strobel book. Or Tim Keller's *The Reason for God,* which is pretty good.

B. Try to forget about the intellectual challenge and hope it goes away. Like when your car starts making a weird noise but you don't want to get it checked out, so you turn up the radio and think, *Maybe it'll stop sputtering tomorrow.*

C. Dismiss the information as inaccurate or misguided. Or dismiss the messenger as ignorant or apostate or evil. Just make sure you dismiss *something,* so you sleep better at night.

D. Go hard-core atheism. Weep in despair and discard

      your faith like a winning lottery ticket that turns out to have been completely fake.

E. Embrace skepticism or agnosticism. Hold onto a shred of hope as you seek purpose in life apart from religion.

F. Own up to the doubt and keep moving.

As you might guess, I'm not satisfied with any of the first four answers. Not completely. Occasionally A helps, but only so much. I am all for using one's God-given intellect to search out questions and apply logic to faith. I'm glad Christian apologetics has been helpful for people who wrestled with spiritual questions only to find those answers leading them into — rather than away from — rational faith. But for every C. S. Lewis converting from atheism to Christianity, aren't there other people who turned to Islam or Buddhism or Mormonism using similar arguments? And aren't there people of faith who give it up because the arguments fail to convince?

Apologetics can only take a person so far, and it hasn't taken me far enough. For some people, intellect may be an exit off the doubter's road. For me, it's the center line that keeps me on it.

Option B is worthless. It involves intellectual laziness or assuming a head-in-the-sand position, neither of which is very flattering. Option C seems to be a favorite option of either conservative or liberal fundamentalists—both extremes. But I'm not generally a fan of anything labeled "extreme" unless it's a chocolate dessert or a thrill ride. And the dismissal tactic, in most cases, isn't intellectually honest.

Answer D is a total downer, and the least fun option by far. E is less depressing, but still a huge and painful leap. For me, at least, discarding faith would be like discarding both my legs at the hip. I've been standing on them for as long as I can remember. Faith is part of who I am. It would be deeply wounding to lose it. To return to the metaphor, I would be abandoning my base turtle—the foundation of my entire turtle stack—and starting over with a brand-new one. That's a painfully life-changing reboot.

So I choose F. I almost always choose F. I accept my doubt for what it is. I embrace my humanity and the stumbling faith and limited understanding that come with it. I keep walking despite my limp.

You didn't ask, but here's my theory about what makes a good marriage. Every lasting marriage is built on three things: friendship, honesty, and shared jokes, by which I mean the ability to laugh with each other because of things that no one understands (or finds funny) but you and your spouse.

One of the jokes my wife, Aimee, and I share involves what we call the *horrible, here taste it!* tendency. You've seen it before. Someone drinks or eats something awful, makes a horrible face about it, and then asks their companion to join them in the awfulness. *Blech. This milk expired last Wednesday. It's horrible. Here, taste it!*

So anytime I ingest something nasty, my immediate (and now-ironic) response is to offer it to Aimee. It makes us laugh, but only because we recognize it as a universal tendency. Our natural impulse, when confronted with unpleasantness, is to share that unpleasantness with someone else. Not out of spite or hatred, but out of the need to have someone else corroborate our feelings. I want to know that the expired chocolate milk really is rancid and that you know it's rancid, too.

Shared revulsion is a community builder. It connects people. That's why the best way to view a horror movie — or a shock comedy — is not in isolation at home but in a crowded public theater.

We'll gladly share nervous laughter when a film makes us cringe or scream in horror. But I've always been hesitant to share my spiritual uncertainty.[1] I'd rather face it alone, and I have my reasons: embarrassment; shame; spiritual

---

1. . . . he said while writing a book about his spiritual uncertainty.

pride; concern about my reputation; fear about what my friends or family will think; worry that my doubts will lead to confusion or doubt in others, therefore causing a fellow Christian to stumble.[2]

A few of those reasons are others-oriented and spiritually noble, but mostly they're selfish. They're also dishonest, because they disguise who I really am. Jesus had some strong words for the kinds of religious people who concealed their inner ugliness behind a shiny spiritual exterior. He called them out as "whitewashed tombs." For someone once described as "meek and mild" in old hymn lyrics, Jesus hands out quite a smack-down:

> *Woe to you, teachers of the law and Pharisees, you hypocrites! You are like whitewashed tombs, which look beautiful on the outside but on the inside are full of the bones of the dead and everything unclean. In the same way, on the outside you appear to people as righteous but on the inside you are full of hypocrisy and wickedness. (Matthew 23:27–28)*

2. Romans 14:21 is a favorite go-to verse of any good Southern Baptist when it comes to moral decision making. It's also the reason Baptists never want to be seen smoking, drinking, or going to an R-rated movie. Those activities may not be legitimately sinful — but they could cause those with weak faith "to stumble." However, loading up the buffet tray with a plateful of fried chicken in the presence of a dieter is just fine.

Pharisees? You're a bunch of walking caskets. Here's where we often miss the point, because the Pharisees come across as such villains in the Gospels. The point of Jesus' diatribe against them isn't the fact that they're disgusting on the inside. His condemnation isn't aimed at their uncleanness or wickedness. All of us, to some degree, are less than perfect on the inside. We're sinners, full of doubt or lust or pride or anything else that falls into the "bones of the dead" category.

The imperfection is not the point; Jesus is shooting down the dishonest way the Pharisees try to hide that imperfection behind a lemony-fresh mask of religious purity. They covered themselves in religion to conceal the fact that they were weak and sinful — and in need of religion.

Compare that to Peter in Luke 5, when Jesus first gives him the opportunity to become a disciple. Peter is employed as a fisherman at the time, and he's out working his nets with James and John on the Sea of Galilee. These guys have been at it all night with negligible results, when Jesus shows up and gives them some fishing advice. Peter listens, does what Jesus says, and ends up with a net so full of fish it nearly breaks. Stunned by the miracle, Peter drops to his knees in response. "Go away from me, Lord," he says. "I am a sinful man!" (Luke 5:8).

Jesus responds to this confession with compassion and encouragement. He immediately tells Peter, "Don't be afraid" (v. 10). Peter drops everything and follows Jesus.

Peter's first step of faith is being honest about who he is. It's a powerful moment of self-recognition and authenticity. With his sinfulness front and center, he then takes the next step in pursuit of Jesus.

True religion — authentic spirituality — doesn't need to hide things like doubt, sinfulness, or frailty. In fact, it can't. Real spirituality begins with an admission of our fallen nature. That doesn't mean we glorify our failures or indulge in our sins. But it gives us the freedom to acknowledge they exist, without fear. The best explanation of why this is spiritually necessary comes from the apostle Paul.

Paul concludes his second letter to the Corinthians with a series of passages about how rough his life has been. The guy was a calamity magnet. In 2 Corinthians 11, Paul lists the various and sundry ways he has suffered for his faith, and the sheer quantity of mishaps is so extreme that it's almost funny. He was (in order) flogged, whipped, beaten with rods, brained with rocks, shipwrecked, abandoned in the open sea, homeless, nearly drowned in rivers, accosted by bandits, pursued by his own angry countrymen and also by Gentiles. In cities and in the country, over the land and across sea, Paul faced a regular stream of persecution.

After that, in 2 Corinthians 12, the apostle calls attention to his famous "thorn in the flesh" while taking comfort in the fact that God's grace and power are intensified by his weaknesses. Three times in this chapter he repeats something that I need to hear: It's not good to boast about ourselves, but if we must boast, we should boast about our weaknesses (2 Corinthians 12:5, 9, 10). There is value, he says, in owning up to our failures. To hide or ignore them is unchristian, because God's grace is strongest when we are at our weakest.

The Protestant Reformer (and notable sinner) Martin Luther called this condition *simul iustus et peccator*. It's a Latin phrase that means something like "simultaneously saint and sinner." Beautiful and broken all at once. Righteous and immoral at the same time.

What if authentic spirituality isn't an either/or — clean or dirty, forgiven or sinful, faithful or doubting? What if it's all those things at once? What if it's both/and?

It's the disciples watching Jesus heal a guy with leprosy, then watching Jesus perform a long-distance healing on a centurion's servant, then watching Jesus drive out some evil spirits. And then completely panicking when they go out on the lake and a storm starts rocking their boat.

It's the father in Mark 9:24 saying, "I do believe; help me overcome my unbelief!"

It's Peter walking on water and then sinking into the sea. As he starts to go under, Jesus reaches out to save him. "O ye of little faith," Jesus says, "Why did you doubt?"

I imagine Peter's response was the same one he gave in Luke 5: Remember what I said earlier, Jesus? I am a sinful man. *Simul iustus et peccator.*

We get it, you might be thinking. *You keep throwing around Latin phrases so you'll look smart, and you want us to be honest and real and authentic about our uncertainty. Great idea. So how exactly do we do that?*

That's a good question. At my website, I'm selling T-shirts for $19.95 that say, "My faith is weak today." The best way to be spiritually authentic is to buy one of these and wear it whenever necessary.

If only it were that easy. What does authenticity look like when it comes to doubt? In almost all cases, it looks like humility.

My writing career has given me plenty of opportunities to immerse myself in big theological subjects, like the end times and the book of Revelation. We like black-and-white answers to big religious questions, but I've discovered that the more I learn about a subject, the more shades of gray come into view. Knowledge leads to complications, as the previous chapter made clear. So when it comes to something like the second coming, or the rapture, or the last days, I often have to admit to people that — while I may know a lot of facts about what the Bible says — I'm more clueless than ever about what it means. In conversations about the book of Revelation, I've labeled myself an "eschatological agnostic."[3]

Christians are afraid of the word *agnostic,* but we shouldn't be. An agnostic is someone who believes that the essential nature of something is ultimately unknowable — like the existence of God, for example, or how things might go down in the last days. Within our religious tradition, we might accuse an agnostic of an unwillingness to take that final, important step of faith. In defense, the agnostic simply recognizes that his or her understanding is limited and embraces that fact.

Despite the spiritual baggage that the word *agnostic* carries among Christians, I believe it's healthy and humble to acknowledge that, despite our best efforts and despite our strong faith, some things truly are unknowable. There are few things that turn me off more than people who speak with absolute certitude about complex issues (like eschatology or the Bible) or deep mysteries (like God or the saving work of Christ).

---

3. *Eschatological:* of or related to the last things, the end times, the second coming, etc.

For me, this looks like not being afraid of doubt and not struggling so hard against my lack of understanding. I'm acknowledging that my viewpoint—of what the Bible means in certain places, or of the rightness or wrongness of my faith tradition, or of all the stuff I've been writing about in this book—may be wrong. Or at least incomplete. That's because I'm human.

In *The Myth of Certainty,* a brilliant and encouraging book about spiritual doubt, Daniel Taylor writes, "We should therefore reject self-congratulating narrowness, always seeking a deepening and broadening of our understanding rather than a hardening of it."[4] A doubter keeps his or her understanding deep but soft. Humility is a great softener.

Another authentic way to handle doubt is to keep perspective. Twenty years ago my most intense doubt was about whether or not I was saved. I never spoke of it to anyone. I kept it buried because I'd built up a reputation as a "leader" in my Southern Baptist youth group, which seemed important then but now seems pretty lame. As I read and studied and expanded the narrow focus of my

---

4. Daniel Taylor, *The Myth of Certainty: The Reflective Christian and the Risk of Commitment* (Downers Grove, IL: InterVarsity Press, 1992), 127. If the only accomplishment of my book is encouraging you to read Taylor's book, then I'll be happy.

religious beliefs, I eventually stopped worrying about my personal salvation. My faith, though still wobbly, is deeper now than it used to be. My understanding has grown. That early strain of doubt is far behind me. I've replaced that concern with other doubts.

I mentioned earlier that doubt is seasonal. It comes and goes based on circumstances and moods and whether or not you're studying the possible influence of Zoroastrianism on Christianity. Uncertainty ebbs and flows, and the questions that plague you today may seem unimportant in the future. Someday, maybe, you'll run into some satisfactory answers. Or maybe not. Maybe those questions will slowly move to the margins, and the things that keep you awake tonight will be afterthoughts a few years from now.

Wait. Be patient. Pray. Trust. Like David in Psalm 13:1, you can start by gnashing your teeth and crying, "How long, O Lord? Will you forget me forever?" But someday you may find yourself admitting, "I trust in your unfailing love" (v. 5).

Owning your doubt also means finding friends who won't let you pretend. My impulse here is to write "Owning your doubt means refusing to pretend." Don't pretend to be better than you are. Don't pretend to be smarter than you are. Don't pretend to be more spiritual than you are. Don't pretend to have it together when you don't. Don't pretend to have all the answers when you don't. Don't pretend to worship when you don't feel like it. Don't pretend.

But I can't write that in good conscience, because I still pretend. A lot. Too much.

And as an image-conscious, still-sinful person, there's not a lot inside me to keep me from pretending. Instead, I find the best defense against spiritual pretending (and pretension) comes from community. Faith is best lived in the presence of others — close friends who know you and believe in you and care about you too much to let you go on acting like everything's cool when it's not. They don't have to hold the same beliefs as you or be fellow doubters. But they do have to be compassionate and tenacious. They have to be willing to ask you how things are going, listen to your first noncommittal answer ("Fine"), and then ask the necessary follow-up: "No, how are things *really* going?"

My wife and I decided early on in our marriage that when one of us sensed a problem and asked the question "What's wrong?" the other was never allowed to answer "Nothing." Each of us has tried to dodge that question at one time or another, but we've learned that artifice is never effective. We refuse to let each other pretend.

All of us need someone who will faithfully live out Jude 22 — "Be merciful to those who doubt" — but who otherwise will be merciless to us when we try to slide into pretension. Unfortunately, it's a lot easier to talk about vulnerability than to practice it. It's simpler to advocate accountability than to find it, because our individualistic culture frowns on these behaviors. Be vulnerable? It'll make me look weak. Hold someone accountable? Maybe I should just mind my own business.

Vulnerability and accountability don't match up with a culture where the individual is king, because they are the by-products of a life lived in community. They require deep, honest relationships, and those kinds of relationships aren't easy to come by. Sometimes they're not easy to endure, either, because they make us uncomfortable. That's why they're so valuable.

Finally, authentic spirituality means realizing that sometimes doubt can be a strength instead of a weakness. Paul delighted in his weaknesses. He wrote that God's strength was made perfect amid his doubts and failures and difficulties (2 Corinthians 12: 9 – 10).

How does doubt strengthen us? One way is the virtue of firsthand experience. I've proven already that I'm no authority on weightlifting, but I do know that bodybuilders develop strong muscles by stressing those muscles with resistance and repetition. A workout actually damages the muscle tissue. Once the workout is over, the muscle begins to repair itself. With each repair, the muscle grows stronger.

You can't build muscles without work that is painful and slightly destructive in the short run.

My strongest beliefs are those I've wrestled with for years. Doubt keeps me humble, but it also deepens my passion about the things I truly believe.

One of those beliefs is that faith isn't the absence of doubt. It's believing and acting *alongside* your doubts. The author of Hebrews writes that faith is "being sure of what we hope for and certain of what we do not see. This is what the ancients were commended for" (Hebrews 11:1 – 2). The lesson we learn from inspiring patriarchs and infuriating sinners like Abraham or David is that they exhibited hope despite an uncertain outcome, despite not being able to see beyond the limits of their humanity.

If doubt isn't the opposite of faith, then maybe it is faith's companion. The twentieth-century theologian Paul Tillich once described doubt as "an intrinsic element of faith."[5]

Evangelists like to use an old illustration that compares faith in Jesus to sitting in a chair. Faith, they say, means putting your trust in the chair by sitting in it — giving it a chance to hold you up, instead of just believing that it will. You need to progress from knowledge to sitting-in-the-

5. Paul Tillich, *The Essential Tillich: An Anthology of the Writings of Paul Tillich,* ed. F. Forrester Church (Chicago: University of Chicago Press, 1999), 27.

chair belief. (It's your basic Jesus-as-furniture metaphor.) I've heard and seen this illustration time and time again. But personally, I think they're approaching the chair/trust/faith connection from the wrong angle.

I'm writing from a computer chair in my home office. I sat down in this chair without giving it a thought. The question *Will it hold me up?* never crossed my mind because I sit in this chair every day. I have rational certainty that it will not fall apart when I plop into it. Is that because I have faith in the chair? No. I have *knowledge* of the chair. Tested, working knowledge. Practical experience. I can see it, I can feel it, and I can park my butt in it. There is no mystery or uncertainty when it comes to my chair. It doesn't require any faith on my part.

The removal of chair-doubt means chair-faith is entirely unnecessary. Faith and doubt work together. Why, then, do I need to hide my doubt and cover it with fake spirituality? Why fear it? Why agonize over it?

Why not embrace it, own it, live it, boast about it, and let God's grace increase amid my weakness?

That's one reason I feel compelled to write this book. I'm not especially proud of my struggles to believe. I don't glory in them.[6] But maybe, like Paul, I should brag a little

---

6. *Really?* you're thinking. *Exactly how does "not glorying" in your doubt line up with, um, making it the subject of a book?* Touché.

about what a spiritual weakling I am. Because when I try to shove that stuff deep inside where no one will see it, I am living dishonestly. I know there are others just like me who have been through or are going through the same thing. Community is built on shared experience, and pretty much everyone experiences doubt at some time or another. Instead of pretending it doesn't exist, trying to forbid it, or trying to prevent it, maybe we should just let it fly and see what happens together.

Honesty and vulnerability have led to my own spiritual growth. They lead to spiritual growth in others too. In his book *Telling Secrets,* Frederick Buechner opens up about his father's alcoholism and eventual suicide. Exposing his wounds to the world is painful, but in the book's introduction, Buechner argues that it's beneficial.

> *I have come to believe that by and large the human family all has the same secrets, which are both very telling and very important to tell. They are telling in the sense that they tell what is perhaps the central paradox of our condition — that what we hunger for perhaps more than anything else is to be known in our full humanness, and yet that is often just what we also fear more than anything else.*[7]

---

7. Frederick Buechner, *Telling Secrets* (New York: HarperCollins, 1991), 2–3.

Without authenticity about our failures and secrets, Buechner writes, we eventually lose track of who we really are. Instead, we come to accept the glossier public version of ourselves because we think the world will like that image better than the real thing. But fake Jason is never preferable to real Jason. Unless your spouse asks you whether or not she looks fat in a certain outfit, dishonesty is never an acceptable alternative to the truth.

Numbers 11 is a dramatic account of a moment when Moses admits his weakness to God. Moses was dealing with some stress at the time. He'd overseen the construction of the tabernacle. He'd been relaying God's laws to the children of Israel. He'd seen God provide daily sustenance through manna. And yet all he kept hearing was the constant complaining of the Israelites. They were tired of manna. They wouldn't stop whining for the meat, fish, and other foods they'd enjoyed in Egypt.

Eventually, Moses can't handle it any longer, and he blows up. He takes his doubt and anger to God: "Why have you brought this trouble on your servant? . . . I cannot carry all these people by myself; the burden is too heavy for me. If this is how you are going to treat me, please go ahead and kill me" (Numbers 11:11, 14–15).

These are strong words and a bold admission of weakness, failure, and confusion on Moses' part. God responds by raising up seventy of Israel's elders to stand alongside Moses. Their job is to support him in his thankless leadership role. God promises to pour out his spirit on the seventy, just like he has with Moses. "They will help you carry the burden of the people so that you will not have to carry it alone," the Lord says.

When Moses owns his doubt, God comforts him with community. Transparency doesn't just bring Moses closer to God. It saves his sanity.

Self-deception does the opposite. Hiding our doubt pulls us further from God and denies us the blessing of real community. It prevents us from taking the next step toward faith. Like Moses, we need to declare that we're overwhelmed. Like Peter, we need to confess our humanness: *Go away from me, Lord. I'm a sinful, doubt-ridden, faith-challenged man.*

When we do that, we can trust that God is not going to smite us with the shipwrecks and snakebites and scourgings that Paul endured. Instead, God will respond to us the same way Jesus responded to Peter: by not going anywhere, by reaching out his hand and telling us not to fear, by inviting us to follow him, to take the next step along the narrow road behind his Son.

chapter 8

The Paralysis of Weddings and Births

I was fearless until I became a father. The longest eight minutes of my life happened the day I drove my daughter, Ellie, home from the hospital. She was two days old — and I drove like I was ninety-two *years* old. At that point, little Ellie weighed an ounce shy of nine pounds. Pretty stout for a newborn, but still ridiculously fragile. I'd spent the previous forty-eight hours worrying that all the well-meaning relatives and friends and nurses who kept pawing at my daughter's impossibly blonde hair would end up poking her in the eye. Or accidentally crushing her tiny skull.

So when it was time to strap her into the way-too-big infant seat and navigate the treacherous five miles back to our house, I drove with the intensity and defensiveness of the front car in a presidential motorcade — with the president holding a nuclear warhead on his lap.

We arrived home safely. No doubt due to my obsessively

darting eyes, my ten-and-two death-grip on the steering wheel, and my refusal to engage in conversation with my wife for fear it would distract me from my mission.

Since then, I have found parenthood to be a reason to agonize about countless new and previously unknown terrors, including, but not limited to, kidnappers, child predators, open windows, open window blinds, the cords of open window blinds (which could strangle a child if you believe the attached warnings), hacking coughs, wasps, mosquito bites, dog bites, Bagel Bites (childhood obesity is a real problem), too-hot Hot Pockets, Methicillin-resistant *Staphylococcus aureus* (MRSA), household allergens, bicycle accidents, schoolyard bullies, Wii elbow, inappropriate attitudes learned from television shows or children's literature, teenage sexuality, potentially ugly body piercings, terrorism, and premature death (mine or theirs). In no particular order.

It's hard out there for a worried parent.

Becoming a parent is one of the most uncertain things you can do in life. The cost of raising a child from birth to age seventeen is something like a quarter of a million dollars. The time you'll invest in it is worth even more. The emotional investment is so high I wouldn't even attempt to calculate it, even if it were possible to assign a dollar amount to things like frustration, bewilderment, or outright weeping. As a parent, I have a sobering amount of responsibility for how my kids grow up, how they interact with the world, and what kinds of adults they'll become.

And yet some parents do everything right — buy the right toys, read the right books, enroll their kids in the right schools, and offer just the right amount of discipline and encouragement and educational videos — and still their kids end up being little jerks. Or worse, you could invest all those emotions and time and money in a kid who turns out better than you ever hoped, only to see his or her life cut short due to tragedy.

All that work, all that love, all that heartache … and nothing to show for it. There is no greater joy than becoming a parent — nothing makes me happier than jumping on the trampoline with both of my kids. Individually, I love talking about books with Ellie. I love my light saber battles with Owen. But in the same breath, I'll tell you there's nothing as frightening as parenting these two.

This isn't surprising. We've all known (or been) rebellious kids. We've known kids who died too early. We've known kids who've gone off the deep end. We've known grieving parents. Parenthood is a monumental risk.

Aimee and I knew this when we decided to have kids. While we understood the theoretical hazards, we knew the potential rewards were far, far greater. We made a choice to become parents. Once we made that choice, we stuck to it. After all, you're either a parent or you're not. It's a 100 percent commitment. You can't be sure of anything — except that once you become a mom or dad, you will never be the same.

Marriage is the same way. You meet someone, you fall in love, reach a point where you can't imagine life without the other person, and make a choice. You decide to commit. In sickness and in health, in times of joy and in times of sorrow, 'til death do you part. You say "I do," and then you're married — all the way. No one gets kinda married. You're either in or you're out.

And yet . . . your young, highly intelligent, and competent wife could become a totally different person once the honeymoon's over. I've known at least a couple of guys who married someone only to see her completely change — and by change I mean "turn crazy" — by the end of the second year of marriage.[1] They're divorced now.

Or your thoughtful, loving fiancé could end up being one of those guys who begins to love his career and his Blackberry way more than he loves you. He could have an affair with that hot barista with the pierced eyebrow. He

---

1. No sexism intended. I'm sure some married guys become someone else once the vows are taken too. It's just that, of the two couples I've known, the troubled ones have been wives.

could explode with selfishness when you have children, and leave you when you need him most.

Your wife could fall in love with an old flame she rediscovered on Facebook. She could get so wrapped up in her career—or your kids—that she stops caring for you altogether. She could be wonderful to you but horrible to your family and everyone else, making your life miserable.

Or your spouse could die, which is what happened to my childhood friend, Mike. A couple years ago, Mike became a widower and a single dad overnight. His wife died of a rare set of medical complications that came out of nowhere a few days after childbirth. She left behind a four-year-old girl, a newborn son, and a grieving husband. The way Mike has endured such tragedy impresses me to no end. But when I think about his loss and that of his kids, my heart breaks.

Like parenting, the act of marriage is a blind step into the fog of uncertainty. All you can be sure about is each individual action along the way—buying a ring, picking a honeymoon destination, closing on that first house—but beyond that lies the unknown. When you get married, you hope for the best. You act upon a combination of reason and guts and undying love. You trust. You can't see the bottom, but you step off the cliff anyway.

With all the terrible things that *could* happen after

getting married or having kids, it's a wonder any of us ever ties the knot or brings a child into the world. Why does anyone make a lifetime-defining choice that's so fraught with the potential for being wrong, or for getting hurt, or for absolute failure? Why do some people make this choice without (it seems) much thought at all to what they're getting into? How are we all not just paralyzed with indecision when it comes to weddings and births?

It's because we see the potential for something wonderful. The possibility of finding meaning and purpose and love and companionship is worth the risk because uncertainty can't compel us like hope can. Writer and pastor John Ortberg says it well: "Trust is better than certainty because it honors the freedom of persons and makes possible growth and intimacy that certainty alone could never produce."[2]

Philosophers have a name for this kind of moment, where we refuse to be intimidated by the unknown, where we have to be decisive despite a total lack of details. It's called a leap of faith.

Unless your business card identifies you as a professor of philosophy, you are not allowed to claim a favorite

---

2. John Ortberg, *Faith and Doubt* (Grand Rapids: Zondervan, 2008), 137.

philosopher. Just FYI. It's pretentious. But if I were forced to choose a favorite philosopher, it would be Søren Kierkegaard, and not just because any name boasting two *K*s, double *A*s, and that weird *O* with the line through it is super cool. Kierkegaard, a nineteenth-century philosopher and theologian, was brilliant beyond belief. You wouldn't have wanted to spend too much time with him though, because he was also fairly depressive. If he were still kicking around today, he would have black-painted fingernails, deliberately unkempt hair, and a heavy rotation of The Smiths on his iPod.

Kierkegaard knew firsthand the uncertainty of life and the risks of love. His mom died right after he turned twenty-one. Four of his brothers and sisters died before that. At the age of twenty-seven, Kierkegaard proposed to his longtime love, Regine Olsen, of whom he once said, "I will cast everything from me in order to be light enough to follow thee."[3] But he called off the engagement a year later, convinced that he was too melancholy to make a good husband—or something like that. (The reasoning behind the broken engagement has always been hazy.) At any rate, Kierkegaard couldn't bring himself to take that step into the unknown. Regine ended up marrying someone else, but

3. Alexander Dru, ed. *The Soul of Kierkegaard: Selections from His Journals* (Mineola, NY: Dover Publications, 2003), 62.

Kierkegaard remained fixated on her. It's widely accepted that the repercussions of his romantic failure resonated through everything he wrote.[4]

I'm bringing this up because Kierkegaard gets credit for introducing the phrase "leap of faith" to the English lexicon, even though he was Danish and even though his concept is more accurately described as a leap *to* faith.

As overly thoughtful philosophers tend to do, Kierkegaard divided life into multiple spheres of existence. One was the aesthetic sphere, which involved the instant choices and mundane experiences we face every day. The second was the ethical sphere of morals and values. Unlike the instant stuff, these morals were not mundane but eternal. Yet neither of those spheres, Kierkegaard believed, were sufficient when it came to finding meaning in life. Neither a temporal dedication to the present moment nor a commitment to timeless values could satisfy. We needed something else.

In Kierkegaard's opinion, that something else was religion. And specifically, he considered that religion to be Christianity, where the temporal met with the infinite in the person of Jesus Christ. This idea wasn't exactly revolutionary, since his native Denmark was a fairly Christian

---

4. This explains the happy-go-lucky titles of his books, including *The Sickness unto Death*, *The Concept of Anxiety*, *Fear and Trembling*, and that notable party favorite *The Concept of Dread*.

place already, with plenty of churches and outwardly religious citizens. But the external religiosity annoyed Kierkegaard greatly. He looked at the nation of Denmark and saw a bunch of people who called themselves Christians without thought or commitment. They believed they were Christians because they lived in Denmark, and Denmark was a Christian place. In Kierkegaard's opinion, Danish Christians were unchallenged, shallow, and completely uninterested in the kind of personal transformation that Jesus called for in the Gospels.

For the faithful of his day, Christianity was the religious system you entered at birth. You stuck with it by thinking the right things. It was rational and easy. Kierkegaard thought this was stupid, because clearly some aspects of Christianity didn't match up with plain logic. Jesus was fully God and fully man, all at the same time? The Godhead is three persons — the Trinity — in one? Those statements don't lend themselves to a nice clean diagram.

Kierkegaard couldn't just ignore these problems like everyone else. To fully embrace a belief in God and an acceptance of the Christian religion, he had to figure out what to do with these gaps in logic. He couldn't bridge them, because how can one build a bridge from a location of certainty to another location that can't actually be proved or fully understood? It's like attempting to build a highway that begins in Key West and ends at the back door of heaven.[5]

So Kierkegaard, the deep-thinking Dane, decided the only way to get from reason to faith was to jump.

This leap occurred, Kierkegaard wrote frequently, in "fear and trembling."[6] It was a risk. It was a step past the borders of knowledge and beyond common sense. It offended the basic intelligence and reason that characterized Enlightenment-era philosophy. But Kierkegaard believed that in order to fully experience the religious life, the leap must be taken deliberately. Despite the uncertainty, despite the hesitancy, despite the inability to reconcile doubts, despite the lack of a guaranteed outcome, true religion required action.

Kierkegaard's leap to faith was not a calculated risk or a temporary form of trust. He viewed it as an eternal decision made with 100 percent commitment. The choice was nonnegotiable and binding. Once you made it, there was no going back. Which made the leap to faith not just the choice of a lifetime, he believed, but the apex of human freedom. Life was not a series of soft transitions between

---

5. Of course, a lot of Christians would argue that Key West is the last place anyone would want to build a bridge to heaven.

6. This phrase comes from Philippians 2:12, where the apostle Paul advises the recipients of his letter to "continue to work out your salvation with fear and trembling."

Kierkegaard's "spheres," from mundane life to ethical values to cultural religion. It required decisive leaps from one distinct location to another.

Kierkegaard jumped into the unknown. So have I.

Why bring up all the woo-woo philosophical stuff? One reason might be that I want you to think I'm smart. But the real reason is that the relationship between faith and doubt in Kierkegaard's philosophy is instructive. A lot of the Christians I know, from regular churchgoers to seminary-trained pastors, tend to approach faith and doubt from an either/or perspective. You have one or the other. Doubt cancels out faith. Faith indicates the absence of doubt.

Kierkegaard thought this mindset was wrong. For him, doubt was an essential part of faith. They were companions. In fact, faith wouldn't even exist if doubt were not also present, because the essence of faith was the leap taken in the face of uncertainty. Faith wasn't a set of beliefs, or an ability to hold onto those beliefs without wavering. Faith was action—action taken right in the middle of your doubts.

If there were no uncertainty at all, a leap of faith wouldn't even be necessary. You could just keep on walking.

In religious faith, as in parenting and marriage, the best response to uncertainty and doubt is commitment. Your kids may occasionally disappoint you, but you love them and raise them anyway, gritting your teeth and hoping for the best. Your spouse may be less than perfect, but you commit to a lifetime of companionship anyway, loving sacrificially and praying for grace. Your relationship with God may be full of doubt, but you leap to faith and hope it's all real. You worship. You gather with other believers. You pray for mercy.

In my life, I struggle with the paralyzing nature of doubt. Why pray if I don't know what good it does? Why lead my small group if I have serious questions about the subject matter? Why address a congregation in a sermon if I'm not even close to figuring anything out? Religious doubt makes me want to sit back and do nothing.

But what if I extended this hesitancy beyond my spiritual life and into my family life? We love to go out for breakfast on the weekends, but isn't there always the chance one of my kids could choke on a cinnamon roll or get food poisoning? We love to vacation in the mountains of New Mexico, but what if we had a terrible accident on the way there? My wife and I still fly together on airplanes, despite imaginations that run wild with horrible potential outcomes. If our plane crashed, who would care for our kids?

I have a wonderful marriage. I have smart, fun, enjoyable kids. Despite my spiritual uncertainty, I have a great life. But I can't say tomorrow will arrive without a doubt. I can't know that everything will stay great forever. But I live as if it will.

Every day, in the face of uncertainty, I can either do nothing or I can do something. I procrastinate. I choose to do something. I do stuff. I save for retirement and for my kids' college. I plan vacations.

We all do. We go on living. We commit.

Doubt is a condition of humanity, but doubt is no excuse for inaction. If you wait until all doubt is gone before you decide to have kids or get married, you'll end up childless and alone and surrounded by too many cats. If you wait until all doubt is removed before you follow God, you'll never take that first step of faith. You wouldn't need to.

My church has long had a ministry to "special adults," a group of several dozen church members who are mentally disabled. Many of them, of course, have other disabilities as well, from cerebral palsy to Down syndrome to blindness. That said, their Sunday school classes are by far the most joyful place to be on Sunday mornings. When I was in high school, I used to lead music every weekend for their classes. It was the easiest and most fulfilling volunteer work I've ever done. I didn't have to be a good guitarist (which I wasn't) or singer (ditto). The only requirement was remembering the words to "I'll Fly Away" and "Amazing Grace" and "Jesus Loves Me."

Their faith was childlike, exuberant, and infectious, and I'll break the writerly injunction against using clichés by saying I received more from serving them than they ever got from me.

Several months ago, our church baptized one of the members of this group by immersion, and I can't stop thinking about the circumstances of her baptism. Some may be offended at the notion of immersing someone of severely limited intelligence, but our church views baptism as a public testimony of a person's decision to follow Christ. With a childlike faith, she knew that God loved her. She knew that she loved Jesus too, and she wanted to make it public.

As her Sunday school teachers and our pastors attempted to explain baptism to her, they could tell that she was nervous about the experience — but serious about going through with it. They told her it symbolized Jesus dying (going under the water) but rising again to new life (coming back out of the water). She nodded like she understood, but she kept asking questions like "Will it hurt?" and "What will it feel like?" They reassured her that no, it wouldn't hurt. She would only get wet and be under the water for a second.

When it came time to baptize her, due to her disability, the pastor needed three helpers to carry the woman into the baptistery. The four of them held her in a fireman's carry as the pastor introduced her and told a little of her story. She was still very nervous. At one point, she leaned over to one of the guys and asked, loudly, "Am I going to drown?" He shook his head. No, of course not.

The pastor eased her backward into the water and immediately brought her up. She came back out, sputtering a little, and immediately asked, "Did I die? Did I die?"

The guys didn't know what she was talking about. They carried her out of the baptistery and got her to the dressing room, where her caretakers helped her get dressed. They later learned that this woman hadn't quite grasped the fact that her baptism was only *symbolic* of death and resurrection. She thought it was literal — that she would die when she went beneath the water but would come back to life again. Just like Jesus.

And she was willing to do it. She simply wanted to know whether or not it would hurt.

I don't know how to feel about this story. On one hand, I feel horrible about the fear she must have experienced. Even thinking about it now makes me *really* uncomfortable. On the other hand, I'm inspired by her willingness to be baptized — to profess her beliefs in such a public way — despite her assumption that it would require her death.

But mostly I feel moved by her profound faith. It

compelled her to take a step toward something that went far beyond the limits of her intellect and reason. She was afraid. She didn't fully understand. But rather than wait for certainty, she got wet. In faith she was lowered down, and in faith she rose up.

chapter 9

Faith with a Kung Fu Grip

In 1974 Hasbro released a brand-new version of its popular G.I. Joe toy that featured a game-changing innovation: the "Kung Fu Grip." Instead of his usual immobile meathooks — pretty much good for nothing but karate chops — this soldier had little rubber hands curled up into a loose fist. The soft, flexible fingers allowed him to grip a handgun or brandish a stick. Now he could hold onto a rope while climbing up a mountain. He could swing from a helicopter. He could dangle from a tree. On YouTube, you can watch one of the original TV commercials advertising the Kung Fu Grip, and it shows G.I. Joe attacking and grabbing a snake.

This G.I. Joe was different. He wasn't passive. He didn't just sit around anymore. He could *do* stuff. The new G.I. Joe with the Kung Fu Grip transformed toy culture because he was no longer simply a masculine doll for boys. He became something far greater: an *action* figure.[1]

I read a lot when I was a kid. Along with Sasquatch encounters, ghost sightings, shark attacks, and the Hardy Boys, one of the subjects that really captured my imagination was the world of daredevils and record-breakers. Real-life action figures. One of them was the French tightrope-walker Jean Francois Gravelet — otherwise known as the "Great Blondin" — who gained worldwide fame by crossing Niagara Falls several times in the summer of 1859. According to the stories, thousands of onlookers would gather to watch him traverse 2,000 feet across a three-inch rope while the falls thundered nearby and rapids churned 160 feet below him.

Blondin didn't just tiptoe, either. He crossed the rope with panache. Sometimes he would sit down in the middle of the stunt, or lie down on his back, or do a somersault. Once he crossed with his arms and legs shackled. Another time, he pushed a wheelbarrow across with a stove inside. Halfway across the rope, Blondin stopped, lit the stove, cracked open a couple of eggs and cooked an omelette, which he then lowered on a rope to people waiting in a boat

---

1. Another big innovation to the 1974 G.I. Joe was "lifelike hair." Unfortunately, the hair improvement always played second-fiddle to the Kung Fu Grip. Good thing, because "Faith with Lifelike Hair" would be a really odd chapter title.

below. Someone in the boat ate the eggs, and Blondin continued across. Dude was flamboyant.

One story has Blondin stirring the crowd into a frenzy immediately after completing one of his dramatic crossings. As the onlookers cheered, Blondin prodded them. "Who among you believes I can cross back over yet again?" he asked. The crowd roared with applause. "Who among you believes I can cross while carrying a man upon my back?" More clapping and approval.

Yay, Blondin! Of course you can! You're awesome!

He silenced the whoops of adulation and asked one more question. "Which of you would like to be that man?"

(Crickets.)

Eventually, as the story goes, one man raised his hand and volunteered to ride across on Blondin's back.[2] Everyone had faith in Blondin's ability to walk across Niagara Falls on a tightrope. But no one was willing to act on that faith.

I'll be honest: had I been in the crowd that day, there's no way I would have volunteered to ride the Great Blondin across the falls. Not a chance. Because despite his confidence and charisma, despite having just seen proof of his

---

2. It should be noted that this is where the details get foggy. In some stories the nameless volunteer rides on Blondin's back. In others, the volunteer gets pushed across in a wheelbarrow. We do know for sure that, at least on a couple of occasions, a man named Harry Colcord crossed the falls on Blondin's back. (He was Blondin's manager.)

abilities with my own eyes, despite the emotional surge produced by his presence, there was still too much uncertainty and danger in the situation. Sure, I might get a free omelet out of it, but I could die too. I would have been paralyzed with doubt, hesitation, and fear — just like all those other members of the Blondin Fan Club (Greater Niagara Chapter).

Faith wasn't the belief that Blondin could walk across the rope in safety, because everyone *believed* he could do it. In fact, they *knew* it. They'd already seen him do it. Faith was the ability to *act* on that belief, to step forward despite the uncertainty, to volunteer to let some crazy French guy tote you across a cascading cataract of death.

Or, to return to a previous story, it's the willingness to be baptized even if you think it might kill you.

In the face of doubt, faith is best expressed through action. The two are partners in our pursuit of God. Faith calls for action, and action gives feet to faith.

"Faith by itself, if it is not accompanied by action, is dead," wrote James in his New Testament letter. "But someone will say, 'You have faith; I have deeds.' Show me your faith without deeds, and I will show you my faith by what I do" (James 2:17 – 18).

Remember the disciples who encountered the post-resurrection Jesus on the mountaintop? They saw him, live and in person, according to Matthew 28. And when they did, they worshiped him. I'm not the best Christian in the world, but I'm pretty sure worshiping Jesus is the correct response when confronted, face to face, with the risen Christ.

Not all of them worshiped, though, according to Matthew's gospel. "But some doubted," says verse 17. When given the choice to worship or not, at least a few of the disciples chose the less pious option B.

Notice how Jesus responded to their doubt. He didn't scold them. He didn't whip out a scroll of Daniel to walk them through the Old Testament stuff about resurrection. He didn't sigh dramatically and perform yet another miracle to display his spiritual clout. He didn't remind them of his messianic credentials. He didn't drop what he was doing to pray for them. He didn't wave his tunic at them, Benny Hinn-style, to magically infuse them with the power of belief or deliver them from demonic influence. He didn't bust out a PowerPoint presentation on the historical reliability of his death and resurrection, using tiny little crosses in place of bullet points.

Jesus pretty much ignored their doubt and did something else instead: he gave them an assignment, otherwise known as the Great Commission. He told them to go and make disciples of all nations. He told them to baptize new believers and teach those believers to obey the things he had taught (Matthew 28:19 – 20). Live it out. Don't let your doubts stop you from living in faith.

In the face of serious doubt, Jesus didn't flinch. When his disciples were stricken with doubt during a literal mountaintop experience with Jesus, at the apex of his three years of ministry, Jesus countered his followers' doubt by telling them to take action.

During my seasons of doubt, this passage informs my faith more than anything else in the Bible. I've learned that the best response to doubt is to take seriously Jesus' response to the disciples: to use my kung fu grip. To go do stuff.

In the Bible, this doubt-action pattern isn't confined to the post-resurrection mountaintop, either. In John 20, when Thomas refuses to believe that Jesus really has risen, Jesus approaches the doubter and speaks directly to him. "Put your finger here; see my hands," he instructs Thomas (John 20:27). Do this. Take action.

It shows up with Moses. When God tells Moses his whole plan for rescuing his people from the Egyptians, Moses hesitates. Even though the plan is mystically delivered via a talking, burning bush — which would have been supernatural enough to get *my* attention — the shepherd isn't so sure. He's worried about being a spokesman for the Almighty, so he asks the bush, "What if they do not believe me or listen to me?" (Exodus 4:1). In answer to Moses' doubt, God gives him instructions. He tells him to throw his staff on the ground. It becomes a snake. God tells him to pick up the snake. It turns back into a staff. He tells Moses to put his hand inside his cloak. The hand comes out all nasty and leprous. Then he puts it back in, pauses, and pulls it back out. The hand is clean. Do this. Take action.

When the angel of the Lord appears before Gideon and informs him that he's been chosen to save Israel from the Midianites, Gideon does a double-take. He just can't see it happening. His clan is weak. He personally is the least impressive guy in his family. Ask anyone: Wheat farmers make lousy warriors. But in answer to Gideon's doubt, the angel gives him instructions. He tells him to arrange his offering of meat and unleavened bread in a certain way on a rock. When Gideon does this, out of nowhere, a fire flares up around it. Do this. Take action.

When Elijah flees for his life after having been threatened by Jezebel, he parks himself under a tree in the desert and prays for his life to end. As mentioned earlier, this is right after an amazing display of God's power on Mount Carmel — the whole dramatic, victorious, fire-from-heaven encounter with the prophets of Baal — yet Elijah is wracked with depression, despair, and doubt. He asks God to end his life. In reply to Elijah's doubt, the angel of the Lord appears and tells Elijah, you guessed it, to do something: wake up, eat, and get moving toward Mount Horeb. On the mountain, Elijah complains again about his sorry state. God gives him another assignment. Go to Damascus. Anoint new kings. Appoint a successor. Do this. Take action.

But what does this action look like for us doubters? What does a doubt-plagued Christian life look like? How can we stop wringing our hands in despair and start *living*?

When it comes to following the teachings of Jesus and the traditions of Christianity, I have decided not to let my doubt paralyze me. I'm going to climb into Blondin's wheelbarrow and see where it takes me. So I do Christian stuff. I study the Bible. I talk to my kids about God. I pray with them. I pray alone. I read books about my faith. I play the drums for the worship team at my church. I lead a small group. I write articles for religious magazines. I write books about religious subjects. I blog about faith. I'm passionate about social justice, and I try to use my writing platform to call attention to ministries and causes I support. Sometimes I even preach.[3]

Whoa, you're thinking. *That's a lot of super-spiritual*

---

3. This is always difficult, and yes, sometimes I feel like a hypocrite. But if God can use screw-ups like Moses and Elijah and the disciples for his purposes, he can theoretically use me too. (I end up preaching a lot about doubt and failure and grace.)

churchy stuff. What about people who doubt so much we can't even attend church? Writing books and preaching is way off the table for us.

You're right, of course, and that's half my predicament right there: I'm immersed in church culture. What about those whose doubts have pulled them away from church attendance and Christianity altogether? Doubt caused discomfort with church, discomfort turned into a resistance to spiritual things, resistance morphed into religious inertia, and now Sunday brunch is one of your favorite things in the world. Give it up for a faith you half-believe in? No way!

My advice to you is to take small, deliberate steps toward faith. Find a way to pray, even if you can't manage more than a humble *thank you.* Add some spiritual flavor to your reading list, whether it's a book or a blog.[4] Seek out understanding believers and engage them in conversation. Drop by a church service or two (for the Sunday-morning challenged, there are a lot of churches that worship on Saturday or Sunday evenings). If you're not comfortable enough to participate, then sit in the back and just observe. Listen. Watch. Better yet, find a church that's active in your community and volunteer to serve alongside them. Most likely they won't make you fill out a doctrinal survey

4. I recommend fellow doubters Michael Spencer at www.internetmonk.com and Gordon Atkinson at www.reallivepreacher.com.

before you dish out soup or distribute sandwiches. They'll just be happy to have a warm body and a smile.

Whatever you do, stop doing nothing about your faith. Do something. Take action.

In a great little old book called *The Seven Deadly Virtues,* the now-retired Baptist preacher Gerald Mann compared faith to riding a bicycle. "You're either on or you're off," he wrote. "There's no stopping, or you're dead."[5] Once you quit moving, quit discovering, quit living the Christian life, then you're likely to topple to the ground.

So I try to keep pedaling, even when I'm doubting. I keep living as a committed Christian, even on the days when I don't feel like one. Even on the days when the agnostic side of the faith spectrum looks pretty inviting, even on the days when doubt takes hold and shakes me to the core, I keep moving. I keep living as if the sun will rise, as if I'll survive the waters of baptism, as if Jesus will indeed carry me safely across the falls. That's me in the corner, trying not to lose my religion. How? By working out my salvation with fear and trembling.

I show my faith by what I do.

---

5. Gerald Mann, *The Seven Deadly Virtues* (Waco, TX: Word Books, 1979), 81.

Wait a second! *you might be thinking.* Are you seriously advocating living an outwardly religious life even when your interior faith isn't that strong? You're talking about portraying something on the outside that isn't necessarily true on the inside. Isn't that what Jesus criticized the Pharisees for doing with all that "whitewashed tomb" stuff you talked about in chapter 7? Isn't that what you condemned with all the talk about honesty and transparency and stuff? Isn't that a works-based salvation, which is the opposite of grace? A little contradictory, don't you think?

Well-played, imagined accuser. Here's why I don't think I'm contradicting myself: The whitewashed religious activity of the Pharisees was used to disguise their ugliness. Their exterior spirituality was a costume worn for the sake of keeping up appearances. My determination to live like a Christian despite the presence of uncertainty isn't so I can hide my doubt or pretend it doesn't exist. Instead, it's something I do to *transform* my uncertainty — and my uncertainty is on full display the whole time.

My actions don't earn me anything. They don't gain me entrance to heaven or a bigger portion of God's love or some kind of extra blessing. But Jesus said, "Follow me," so that's what I'm trying to do — even if the following sometimes gets ahead of the belief.

The writer A. J. Jacobs is a great example of this, though he'd probably be surprised to be used as an example of faith. An *Esquire* editor and nonobservant Jew, Jacobs wrote *The Year of Living Biblically: One Man's Humble Quest to Follow the Bible as Literally as Possible*. It's an entertaining memoir about how Jacobs decided to get to know the history of his religious forebears — and their Christian offshoots — by spending a year observing the rules in the Bible. All of them. He stopped cutting the corners of his beard, ending up with a veritable bird's nest hanging off his chin. He refused to wear clothing of mixed fibers. He attempted to stone an adulterer with tiny, harmless pebbles. He observed a weekly Sabbath from working. He prayed on a regular basis, even though he never fully knew to whom he should address his prayers.

Along the way, Jacobs's adherence to the "rules" of religion began to change him. He became more thoughtful. He turned into a nicer person and a better parent. He didn't end up having any real conversion experience — he remains a self-described "reverent agnostic" — but the book is a fascinating account of the transformative power of commitment to a course of action.

Especially telling is the effect of gratitude on his life. In obedience to verses about thanking God for blessings received from the land, Jacobs describes going through an elaborate series of thank-you prayers while eating pita bread and hummus. To paraphrase, he prayed, "Thank you for the farmers who grew the chickpeas to make this hummus. Thank you for the workers who packaged it, and the truck drivers who delivered it, and the employees who stocked it." He writes about how those prayers transformed the act of eating for him. No longer was he able to mindlessly consume something. The actions of thankfulness made him more thoughtful. They connected him more deeply with the world around him. At the end of the project, as he contemplates how his biblical year will affect his future, he gets stuck on the gratitude part: "I'll keep on saying prayers of thanksgiving. I'm not sure whom I'm thanking, but I've become addicted to the act of thanking."[6]

John Ortberg's recent book *Faith and Doubt* contains a wonderful suggestion for those living in spiritual uncertainty. Even though many aspects of our faith may remain unknown or mysterious, God doesn't require us to contort our minds into believing something our human nature finds difficult to believe. He doesn't cram us into faith like a square peg into a round hole. Nor does he want us to force

6. A. J. Jacobs, *The Year of Living Biblically: One Man's Humble Quest to Follow the Bible as Literally as Possible* (New York: Simon & Schuster, 2008), 329.

ourselves into certainty. "What matters then," Ortberg writes, "is not certainty, but faithfulness."[7] Maybe all God requires of us is that we remain faithful to the things we *are* certain about.[8]

Faith isn't obligatory, mindless agreement with theological systems or biblical interpretations. Instead, it's a commitment to acting on the things we know for sure.

Jesus said all we needed was the faith of a mustard seed. I suspect my mustard seeds are those things I know without a doubt. These are the things I'm clinging to with a kung fu grip.

This got me thinking: What *are* the things in Jesus' message that I am certain about? I started with the Sermon on the Mount, which seemed like a good place to find moral instruction and suggestions for action. These are the things I believe in with certainty:

- I believe that the kingdom of heaven belongs to the poor and that the meek will inherit the earth. I believe that those people on the outskirts of society — the sick, the hurting, the disempowered, the

---

7. John Ortberg, *Faith and Doubt* (Grand Rapids: Zondervan, 2008), 149. This is an excellent book about doubt. In fact, I recommend putting my book down and picking up Ortberg's as soon as possible. The book has been republished in softcover with the title *Know Doubt*.

8. Credit Ortberg for this idea. I heard him say something like this in a sermon related to his book, but I didn't find the exact statement in the book itself.

outcast — have a special place in God's kingdom and should be treated with compassion by the followers of Jesus. (Matthew 5:3 – 6)

- I believe a commitment to righteousness, mercy, purity of heart, and peacemaking is something God values and will somehow reward. (Matthew 5:7 – 10)

- I believe a life spent following Jesus really is a light in a dark world. It gets people's attention, it illuminates and helps people navigate the world around them, and it dispels darkness. (Matthew 5:14 – 16)

- I believe that the best individual response to evil is to turn the other cheek and hand over my cloak and walk a second mile, despite having no idea how to apply it in a community or national setting. (Matthew 5:38 – 42)

- I believe that it's good to love your neighbor. It's even better to love your enemies. (Matthew 5:43 – 48)

- I believe that the best "acts of righteousness" are the invisible ones that you never get credit for. I believe that it is important to be generous to the needy, whether that generosity means giving money, stuff, or time. (Matthew 6:1 – 4)

- I believe that prayer is personally transformative, spiritually helpful, and somehow effective, even though I don't understand why or how. But it's clear that Jesus was an advocate of prayer, and you can't go wrong by sticking with the prayer he gave his disciples. (Matthew 6:5 – 14)

- I believe we should forgive the sins of others. (Matthew 6:15)

- I believe there is benefit to fasting — spiritually, physically, and psychologically — but it's not necessarily something you should announce with trumpet fanfare. (Matthew 6:16 – 19)

- I believe there are more important things in life than being rich or successful. Spiritual "treasure" is worth more than monetary or material treasure every time. (Matthew 6:19 – 24)

- I believe that worrying is a good way to miss out on the joys of life and is usually a waste of time. I believe tomorrow will take care of itself, so it's better to live in and fully enjoy the present moment. (Matthew 6:25 – 34)

- I believe that seeking the kingdom of God should be high up on our priority list, and that a life lived with eyes open to God's work in the world is the best kind of life. (Matthew 6:33)

- I believe that God is aware of and moved by the suffering of his children. I want to believe that God will provide for his children, as the passage says, but a realistic glimpse at impoverished or persecuted Christians around the world tells me that my idea of "providing" and God's idea of providing aren't necessarily the same. (Matthew 6:25–34)

- I believe it's best not to judge others, because I'm sinful enough that any kind of stone-throwing is just plain laughable. I have planks coming out of my eyes at all angles, so I'd rather deal with people by showing too much grace than too much judgment. (Matthew 7:1–5)

- I believe that the others-oriented focus of the Golden Rule — doing unto others as you would have them do unto you — doesn't just sum up the Law and the Prophets but is the height of human morality. Christian or otherwise, you can't go wrong living by this creed. (Matthew 7:12)

- I believe that our Christianity is determined less by what we say or claim and more by the fruit we produce, otherwise known as the stuff we do. (Matthew 7:15–23)

- I believe a person who follows the teachings of Christ is well prepared to weather the whole gamut of human storms: from grief, to heartache, to failure, to disappointment. There are few stronger foundations for dealing with life's challenges. (Matthew 7:24–27)

- Stepping briefly outside the Sermon on the Mount, I believe that actions of following Jesus can be best summed up by the Greatest Commandment (Matthew 22:36 – 40), that there is something powerful about sharing the bread and the wine of communion with fellow believers in Jesus Christ (Luke 22:19 – 20), and that grace is a radically life-changing idea in a world that operates on karma.[9]

I have no doubt that these things, which were taught and modeled by Jesus, are true. I also know that their relationship with faith is a synergistic one. Loving others, serving others, and forgiving others are actions that are generally taken as a *result* of faith. But they are also actions that, when pursued, will deepen and even sustain faith.

Many people were shocked by *Come Be My Light,* a collection of letters written by Mother Teresa. The letters — written to her superiors over several decades — weren't what anyone expected from the "Missionary of Calcutta" and the faith-hero of millions. Why? Because they were about Mother Teresa's spiritual darkness. They were about her constant struggles with doubt. She had lived and died as an icon of good works, but her faith was marked

---

9. This isn't a complete list by any means. I could go on, of course, but I've limited it to the Sermon on the Mount for reasons of brevity.

by intense periods in which she felt completely distant from God and even doubted his existence.

In 1946, Teresa received a mystical "calling" from Jesus to abandon her role as a teacher and move to the slums of Calcutta, where she was to tend to street children and dying beggars. The calling was accompanied by visions in which, she wrote, Jesus spoke to her personally and asked her to do his work. They were intense experiences of God's love and direction, and Teresa immediately began the process of following that call. After months of seeking permission at almost every level of the Catholic Church's hierarchy, from her spiritual director to her Indian bishop, and eventually, all the way to Rome, she took to the streets of Calcutta in August of 1948.

The doubts seem to have begun almost immediately. Loneliness. Spiritual darkness. Feelings of despair and isolation and the absence of God. She writes things like "How long will our Lord stay away?" and "Within me everything is icy cold."[10] She admits at one point that prayer was difficult for her. She says she understands the tortures of hell because she has grown accustomed to living without God. She questions the reality of heaven.

These struggles weren't fleeting; they last until her

10. Mother Teresa and Brian Kolodiejchuk, eds., *Come Be My Light: The Private Writings of the Saint of Calcutta* (New York: Doubleday, 2007), 158, 163.

death in 1997. Toward the end she indicates that she has become comfortable with the darkness.

But still. That's a half-century of spiritual doubt from one of the modern world's foremost examples of faith. Yet despite everything she was experiencing — despite feeling abandoned by God in her spirit and actually questioning his existence in her mind — Teresa managed to perform some of the greatest works of charity any of us will ever know. She held dying orphans in her arms. She washed the wounds of lepers. She held the hands of beggars. She and her Missionaries of Charity became famous for their work. She won the Nobel Peace Prize in 1979. On the outside, she never released her grip on what she was supposed to be doing. Like a wrinkled pit bull in a white-and-blue sari, she bit down hard on the calling she had received and clung to it despite the doubt she felt on the inside.

When it came to pursuing the things she knew for sure, Mother Teresa was determined. What does it take to perform the work of Jesus for fifty years, even when you spend that time unsure of his presence and doubting his existence?

It takes faith. An overwhelming amount of faith.

Faith is action. When we act, God uses us despite our doubts and fears and hesitations. Mother Teresa's story gives me great hope. Sometimes my ability to live like a Christian — loving people, serving others, and doing the things I'm certain I should do — may be the closest thing I have to faith.

chapter 10

Unresolved

The famed nineteenth-century Russian pianist Anton Rubinstein was a late sleeper. Often he slept so late that he missed early appointments. This annoyed his wife, so Mrs. Rubinstein came up with a creative method to get him out of bed each morning. She'd go to the family's upstairs piano and pound out a single, dissonant chord. And she'd just leave it hanging in the morning air, unresolved. Anton couldn't stand it—he *had* to resolve that chord. So every morning he would climb out of bed, stumble upstairs, and complete it by playing a nice, pleasant, perfect major triad. The moment Anton departed the bedroom, Mrs. Rubinstein would calmly walk in and make the now-empty bed. Anton was up, and he had to stay up.[1]

Some people really, really need resolution.

---

1. Clifton Fadiman and André Barnard, eds., *Bartlett's Book of Anecdotes* (New York: Little, Brown, 2000), 471. And yes, I realize this is the second illustration using a pianist named Rubinstein. The first, on page 129, involved Arthur Rubinstein, who was Polish and lived in the twentieth century. Apparently I find anecdotes about Rubinstein pianists to be especially meaningful.

If that's you, then I apologize. You're probably waiting for me to tie my musings and concerns and thoughts and stories and suggestions about doubt into a neat little package. Aren't you dying to know exactly how I put all my uncertainty aside and finally —*finally!*— became a hardcore believer?

Don't hold your breath. I'd love to do that for you, but I can't. The doubt is still there. I'm still driving along the Doubter's Road, straining to hear the voice of God through my scratchy A.M. radio and squinting into the darkness ahead.

At this point the best ideas I have for dealing with doubt are already in the rearview mirror. I trust in grace (chapter 3). I pray (chapter 5). I admit my doubt to God and others (chapter 7). I take a Kierkegaardian leap past my reservations and into trust (chapter 8). I try to live in committed obedience to the teachings of Jesus about which I'm certain (chapter 9).

But there is one more thing I do in response to a God who often seems absent or hidden: I keep my eyes open. The focus of this final chapter is the lifelong search for God. It's one of the doubter's most important disciplines.

Let's say you're a piano genius lying in bed. Somewhere in the house, God has played a beautiful, haunting, unresolved piano chord. It startles you awake. It captures your attention. But it also unnerves you. You need to resolve it—the tension pinches your consciousness and won't let up—so you go looking for the source of the music. Only the piano can't be found. Nor can the Piano Player. But the notes of the chord still hang in the air, resonating, echoing off the walls of the house.

Finding the source of the music seems so important that you might just spend the rest of your life searching for the piano, trying to ease the tension.

Spoiler alert, Mr. Rubinstein: You won't succeed. The music won't be resolved in this life. But the process of looking for the piano is worthwhile anyway.

Google has only been around since the late 1990s, but it didn't take long for it to change the world. In 1996 Larry Page and Sergey Brin, two Stanford graduate students, decided to build a better search engine as a doctoral research project. At the time, most search engines simply scoured the Web for keywords, noting the number of times a specific search term showed up on a page. The results were often useless.

Page and Brin wanted a search engine that was more intuitive, one that came up with more relevant results. To make a long, nerdy story short, the secret formulas and search algorithms they came up with were revolutionary. They transformed the Internet. For better or for worse, you almost always find what you want to find when you use Google.

Google allows you to find a needle of information in a haystack that grows exponentially bigger every day. A good search engine makes the infinite finite. It reaches into the chaos of the Web and gives us a small place to stand, a beginning from which to proceed.

There's a good metaphor in there when it comes to dealing with doubt. Do you want to progress toward faith in God? Do you want to make the infinite finite? Start searching. Listen to Jesus:

> *Ask and it will be given to you; seek and you will find; knock and the door will be opened to you. For everyone who asks receives; those who seek find; and to those who knock, the door will be opened. (Matthew 7:7–8)*

I memorized this verse as a kid in Sunday school. It's ingrained in my spiritual brain, generally within the context of "getting saved" or "coming to Christ" or any other evangelistic phrases we might use to describe the experience of choosing to follow Jesus. But until I began thinking about this book, I never realized the uncertainty implied in this passage: Ask. Seek. Knock.

Jesus describes the spiritual life—a life lived in pursuit

of God—with three words that evoke the ideas of searching and mystery. You only ask when you have a question. You only seek when something is missing, or when it's not readily apparent. You only knock on a door when you're on the outside trying to get in.

And yet these are the things Jesus tells his audience to do. Is Jesus aware that a relationship with God is wracked with uncertainty? Is he acknowledging that doubt is central to the pursuit of God? Maybe.

Jesus said, after all, that those who ask will receive. Those who seek will find. Those who knock will be greeted with an open door. That's encouraging stuff, because I can rest in the fact that Jesus promises some kind of resolution to the uncertainty.

But what he doesn't promise is a timeline.

The old philosopher-theologians like Thomas Aquinas and Martin Luther used to refer to God with an excellent Latin phrase, *deus absconditus*. It means the "hidden God." Central to the idea is that God, while personal and omnipresent, is not always located in plain sight. Sometimes he seems remote. Sometimes he seems absent. This is because the idea of an all-powerful, all-present, all-knowing creator God doesn't fit neatly into our human categories. So we tend to think of him as an old man with a long beard—Santa Claus without the red coat and pipe—just to have someone to visualize when we pray. It's hard for us to deal with a hidden God.

But that's how God works. Consider the dramatic conversation between Moses and God at Mount Horeb, described in Exodus 33. Moses, of course, is no stranger to the miraculous presence of God. He facilitated the whole plague thing and led the dry-footed parade across the Red Sea. He followed the pillars of fire and cloud. He even spent time in the "tent of meeting," upon which the cloud of God's presence would descend and Moses and God would speak "face to face, as one speaks to a friend" (Exodus 33:11). I can't imagine what this was like or even what it means, but if anyone was tight with God, it was Moses.

So maybe we should forgive the guy when he starts getting a little more demanding with the Almighty a few verses later. Moses and God are discussing God's presence with the people of Israel, and God announces that he is pleased with his servant Moses. Upon hearing this news, Moses' heart starts beating fast. He takes a deep breath and makes a bold request: "Now show me your glory" (v. 18).

Show me your glory. If you've spent any time in church, that's probably a familiar phrase. It comes up every now and then in contemporary worship songs, mainly because it sounds pious and biblical and because we conveniently forget how God responds to Moses' demand. He agrees to give Moses a glimpse of his goodness. But his glory? Not a chance. "You cannot see my face," he tells Moses, "for no one may see me and live."

Remember that next time you sing the phrase in church. Asking God to show you his glory is like asking for a smiting. It may not be a prayer you want answered.

God compromises with his servant. He gives Moses a fascinating series of instructions that allow him an incomplete glimpse of the Almighty. Moses has to hide in a crack in a rock, covered by God's hand, and only from that protected position is he allowed to observe God's glory. "Then I will remove my hand," God says, "and you will see my back; but my face must not be seen" (v. 23).[2]

So God does reveal himself to Moses, but only in part, and only in small, controlled doses. He remains mostly hidden. If anything, Moses gets to see God's backside—which sounds naughty in a frat-boy sort of way, but which many scholars think is a euphemism for "you can see where I just was" or "you can see where I've been." The best Moses could hope for was not for the fullness of God's presence, but for the echo remaining in God's immediate absence.

This was probably a good idea. I can barely handle a sunrise in the mountains without choking up a little.

---

2. And if in the previous sentence you pictured a gigantic hand sheltering Moses like King Kong scooping up Fay Wray, then you are forgiven.

Seeing my wife and kids after being away from them for a weekend is almost more than I can bear. A vision of God himself, in full glory? None of us could handle it. Neither could Moses.

"Truly you are a God," says Isaiah, "who has been hiding himself" (Isaiah 45:15). Aside from a few experiences — a Nicaraguan trash dump, a living room concert, a teenage conversion to humility — I always seem a step behind God. I see where he's been. I've seen what he does. I've seen lives dramatically changed by Jesus. But very little of it has happened to me live and in person. I've seen brief glimpses of God, bits of glory and slivers of grace, but never the big picture.

This frustrates me, because our world needs the big picture. For all the happy talk about God's blessing and favor on Christian TV, you don't have to look very far to find a God who seems less available than we'd like. Where is God among the AIDS and war orphans of East Africa? Where is God among the victims of terrorism? Where is God in the early death of a young mom from cancer? Where is God among the glitter of Las Vegas and the frenzy of Times Square? Where is God among the piracy of Somalia or the breadlines of Zimbabwe?

I believe God is there. He's just not as visible as we'd like. Maybe he's even shielding us with his hand — like

Moses in the rock — so we don't see too much. If we saw the full picture, we wouldn't need as much faith.

"It is the glory of God to conceal a matter," Solomon wrote. "To search out a matter is the glory of kings" (Proverbs 25:2). We have to stop looking for his immediate activity and instead pay attention to where God has been. It's a matter of adjusting our focus.

Have you ever been in the market for a certain car? As soon as you test drive or research that model, you begin to see that car everywhere. You decide you want a Toyota Yaris and suddenly you're surrounded by Yarises. Or Yarii. Anyway, were there always this many on the road? Where'd those things come from?

Relax. You're not crazy. The sudden proliferation of high-mileage subcompact Japanese cars with silly names isn't due to failing mental health. There's an actual scientific explanation for this phenomenon.

As it turns out, all of us have a little dime-sized cluster of cells near the base of our brain stem called the Reticular Activating System (RAS). It acts as a gatekeeper for incoming information — and our brains definitely need a gatekeeper. All day long we're pelted with sights, sounds, words, music, conversations, advertisements, and other distractions. We'd go insane if our brain tried to process all the stimuli flying past our senses. The RAS protects us by working like an email spam filter. It makes sure the important, necessary stuff lands in your inbox. In other words, it gets your attention and lodges in your brain while the useless stuff slides right on past and gets deleted.

Usually the RAS activates itself automatically, like the way your ears pick up when someone mentions your name, even if you weren't really listening to their conversation. But the RAS can also be tweaked when you need to focus your attention on something new. That's why a certain car seems to become ubiquitous the moment you read about it in *Consumer Reports*. That's why suddenly *everyone* seems to be wearing the jeans you just bought off the clearance rack at Target and why every other nut in the mall seems to be talking on the same kind of cell phone as you. These things had been around you all along, only now your RAS alerts you and you take notice.

Maybe we have trouble seeing God because, as St. Augustine wrote in his *Confessions*, we're not tuned in quite enough: "God is always present to us and to all things; it is that we, like blind persons, do not have the eyes to see."[3]

What if we put our Reticular Activation System to work for us spiritually? What if we began scanning the world around us for the activity of God? What if we decided to

---

3. Quoted in Marcus Borg, *The God We Never Knew* (San Francisco: HarperOne, 1997), 47.

live as a search engine, seeking out the hidden presence of God amid the thousands and thousands of tiny details of our lives? What if the best response to a God who seems absent is to start the process of discovering where he has just been?

My paternal grandfather, John E. Boyett Jr. (we call him Paw-Paw), is a survivor of World War II. Actually, to call him a "survivor" is to make an egregious understatement. He's still alive, but by all accounts, he shouldn't be.

Paw-Paw was a twenty-one-year-old side-gunner and flight engineer on a B–17 bomber, the legendary "Flying Fortress," based out of Italy. On his final bombing run over Austria, his plane was hit by enemy fire. Most of his companions on the plane were killed, but he was able to parachute out. From that point on, he experienced a succession of traumas that should have killed him. These included nearly burning to death as he exited the plane, being hit by shrapnel on the way down, being shot at by a plane-mounted machine gun on the way down (he felt the bullets whiz by his ear), narrowly avoiding a power line as he parachuted down, crashing into a forest, being apprehended by Nazi soldiers and nearly being executed (they argued over whether to kill him immediately or wait), being placed in a prison camp for almost a year and nearly starving to death, being forced into a months-long death march in below-freezing temperatures, and nearly being executed again before getting rescued due to a navigational fluke.[4]

Based on the odds, my grandfather should have died several times over. His survival was miraculous, and by the same token, so is my existence — because my dad and his sisters weren't conceived until after my grandfather returned, wounded, from his captivity. My entire family knows that none of us should be here.

Why did he survive? Paw-Paw tells us today that it's because God had a plan — not for him, exactly, but for us. For my generation. For me, my siblings, our cousins, and our kids. He has lived his life believing he escaped death at every point of the war because God wanted the next generation of Boyetts to follow along. He calls these events his "miracles" and sees the hand of God at work in them.

While some might dismiss his wartime experience as a succession of startling favorable coincidences, Paw-Paw sees God. Others might live through that tragedy and be overwhelmed by the injury, loss, heartache, terror, and discomfort he endured — emotions that, for some, might suggest the absence of God. But Paw-Paw looks back and sees places where God kept showing up to keep him alive.

Rather than leave him broken and bitter, the war inspired my grandfather. It made him a better man. It has

---

4. It's a long, fascinating story, but it's one better told in full somewhere else.

done the same for me too, because it challenges me to make my life count for something. I'm always asking myself: *Is my life worth his survival?*

I can't say without a doubt that God intervened to make sure Paw-Paw survived the war, but I have no other explanations. My family's ability to identify God in the details of my grandfather's capture, captivity, and release has deeply enriched our lives.

When we are deliberate in searching for where God has been, we'll see his activity in surprising places. In the skies above Austria and in a Nazi prisoner-of-war camp. At the gas pump and in the office park. Among the hurting and the successful, the homeless and the jet-setting. In the churches and bars and little league diamonds and big-box store checkout lines. In the struggles and celebrations of our family and friends. In the loneliness of those who have no family or friends. In the middle of our best days and the middle of our worst. On the other end of our phone line or Internet connection. At the gym. In the hospital. On the side of the road. We'll start to see Jesus everywhere, thanks to something called the "incarnation."

More than anywhere else, the "hidden God," *deus absconditus,* becomes visible in the incarnation. In the incarnation, God revealed himself on his own terms, through the person of Jesus Christ. The Creator redeeming his creation by entering into it is one of the central theological concepts behind my Christian faith. The thirteenth-century German mystic Meister Eckhart once said God was like someone who clears his throat while hiding, so he might be more easily found.[5] If that's the case, then Jesus was the loudest throat-clearing ever.

The birth, life, and death of Jesus gets my attention, and it is an audible giveaway I need to hear.

I have to be honest. I am not a Christian because I always like how God is revealed in the Old Testament. Despite the beauty of the Psalms, and power of the messianic prophecies, and the grace-drenched laws meant to help the poor, much of the Old Testament seems primitive and barbaric to me. I don't understand why, in many stories, God seems to come off as a petty, vindictive, violence-prone deity. I don't get why God allows all those horrible things to happen to Job, even though the story ends on a positive note because Job gets a new family and new possessions. That doesn't mean he didn't get universally screwed by God's wager with the Accuser. I absolutely don't understand why the Israelites kept having to slaughter all the men, women, children, and livestock of the tribes who got

---

5. *Meister Eckhart: A Modern Translation*, trans. Raymond B. Blakney (New York: Harper & Row, 1941), 145. The actual quote: "Just as a man who is hiding clears his throat and thus reveals his whereabouts, so it is with God."

in their way — even *if* those tribes worshiped false gods. Chalk it up to inaccurate reporting or anthropomorphizing or my own sinful ignorance, but sometimes I really struggle to love and worship that God.[6]

That struggle doesn't apply to Jesus. I am a Christian because of Jesus. Michael Spencer, an online friend and the popular blogger at InternetMonk.com, once suggested an interesting theory. If you were to place the leaders of all the world's religions in one room and force them to come up with a single person in history who best represented the ideals of their religion, they'd have a hard time doing better than Jesus Christ of Nazareth. Not only does Jesus dispense compassion and grace and mercy, but he confounds his society's expectations. He's the Son of God, intent on redeeming the world and going about his Father's business, but he doesn't do it in the way we expect.

His teachings are revolutionary, but Jesus ends up getting killed before the revolution really begins. And those engineering his death are the very people he's come to save. His disciples are a bunch of undereducated, underage

---

6. Some might argue that this puts me in danger of succumbing to the Marcion heresy, which is named after the second-century theologian who kept trying to separate the teachings of Jesus from the actions of the God of the Old Testament. He went so far as to reject the Old Testament and claim Yahweh to be a separate, less-powerful deity than the God of love revealed by Christ. Marcion was a heretic. I'm not quite ready to go that far.

fishermen with a discouraging tendency to either betray, deny, or ignore their leader.

And yet something happens after Jesus dies. Something big. His ragtag team of failures take his teachings way past their little sect of Judaism, and within a few centuries the Christian faith has come to dominate the Western world. How does *that* happen?

The explosion of Christianity following the death of Jesus is impressive even to nonreligious people. Jesus had power. Moral power, of course, but also spiritual power. And my act of faith is to hope and believe that power was the result of his being exactly who he claimed to be: the Son of the living God. If God in the Old Testament was hidden and confusing and hard to understand, Jesus was live and personal and three-dimensional. He was the Word made flesh, dwelling among us (John 1:14). He was a much clearer picture of who God was and is — right now — and not just where he'd been.

And yet Jesus himself kept returning to the idea of hiddenness. In Matthew 13:44, he compared the kingdom of heaven to a valuable treasure hidden in a field. In the famous "least of these" passage, Jesus says that he can be found in disguise, among the hungry, the thirsty, the stranger, the unclothed, the sick, and the imprisoned. After the resurrection, he enjoyed a long walk and conversation with some of his disciples on the road to Emmaus. These guys were completely bummed, but Jesus kept his identity concealed from them. It took an embarrassingly long time for them to recognize they had been hanging out with the resurrected Jesus. When they finally did catch on, he disappeared again (Luke 24:13–34).

Jesus doesn't show up where he's expected. Sometimes he comes out of nowhere. He appears in places we hadn't thought to look before. Life as a search engine means keeping your eyes open for the fleeting, hidden traces of Jesus. I caught a glimpse in a trash dump in Nicaragua. I had the door opened to me, just a little, when I was a teenager reading Philippians. I've seen Jesus camouflaged in a community of friends, among the too-human failures of the church, and amid the grace that peeks through the cracks of life.

I doubt God's existence more often than I'd like. I read the Bible and somehow end up with more questions than answers. I'm trying to follow Jesus, but I'm afraid my attempts look like a blind man running an obstacle course on an ice rink. But despite the confusion, my goal is to keep moving toward faith rather than away from it. I'm trying to be honest and real. I'm trying to keep my kung fu grip on. I'm trying to keep the search active, and I rest in the hope that my continued searching, in itself, contains a mustard seed's worth of faith.

Let's bring this thing to an end with two related thoughts. One is about having too little. The other is about having too much. Both have something to tell us about the pursuit of God.

Marketing guru Seth Godin once wrote that the best way to keep a business from failing is not to open it in the first place. The best way to keep your bank from being robbed is not to open a bank. The most sure-fire way to keep your email inbox free of spam? You guessed it: Don't open an email account.[7]

A closed-up life is the safest way to live. But it's also boring, unfulfilling, and a few steps shy of turning into the kind of crazy neighborhood recluse who spends all day wearing flannel pajamas, talking to her houseplants, and watching game show reruns.

The best way to live a doubt-free life? Believe too little or don't believe anything at all. Choose the turtle stack of unbelief rather than belief. That might make my life easier, but that's *so* not the kind of existence I want. I'd rather deal with the uncertainty of being too open than suffer through the monotony of a closed-up life. I'd rather risk seeing my hopes get dashed than to choose no hope at all. I'd rather spend life looking for evidence of God — even if finding it

---

7. From Seth's blog (sethgodin.typepad.com), April 23, 2008.

is a struggle—than to conclude, before starting, that there's nothing to see.

I'd rather have a faith that makes me ask too many questions than a faith in which the questions have easy answers (or worse, a religion where questions are forbidden).

We dare not seek too little, but we can also have too much. The writer and literary critic William Dean Howells once wrote a disturbing story called "Christmas Every Day."[8] It's a story within a story, about a young girl who likes Christmas so much she wants it to be Christmas every day of the year. Thanks to the work of the Christmas Fairy, she gets her wish on Christmas Eve. So the next day, she celebrates Christmas—the *real* Christmas—on December 25. She has a great time, then goes to bed. The next morning, *Groundhog Day*-style, she discovers it's Christmas yet again for the girl and her family and apparently the rest of the world. The family thinks this is a strange turn of events, but they chalk it up to a pleasant surprise. Then it's Christmas again on December 27, and on December 28, and so on for a full year of Christmases.

You can guess what happens. After a few months the family grows to hate Christmas. It exhausts them. Waking up to the sight of stuffed stockings by the fire fills them

8. William Dean Howells, *Christmas Every Day and Other Stories Told for Children* (New York: Harper and Brothers, 1892), 3. The story is available as a free ebook at gutenberg.org.

with dread. The endless presents to be opened cause the little girl to break down in tears. People are forced to build barns to hold all the gifts they keep receiving, and before long they just toss them out in the rain. When it becomes clear that the little girl was the cause of the unlimited string of Christmases, the entire nation despises her.

Too much of a good thing was a bad thing.

Could too much of God's explicit presence be a bad thing? Unlike the people who seem to hear from God fifty times a day and talk about spending so much time in his presence, I'm not sure I could handle a constant stream of doubt-busting gifts from God. A few surprises every now and then make it all the more meaningful when I do catch a glimpse of the Almighty.

There is nothing to be gained by having too little of God. And if we had too much of God, as I wrote earlier, we wouldn't need faith. As a doubter, I'm discovering that life in the margin between those two extremes is not such a bad thing after all.

I suspect my travels on the doubter's road haven't been entirely my choice. My skeptical personality seems pre-disposed to doubt. I'm sure the religious environment of my childhood contributed to my uncertainty, despite the well-meaning people behind it. My passion for history and theology are also culprits.

But I've become accustomed to this road. Its twists and turns no longer seem so surprising or its potholes so jarring.

On the doubter's road, I'm driving under the belief — possibly hopeless, but hopefully possible — that it leads me somewhere. Somewhere holy. Somewhere shot through with grace. Somewhere near my eternal home, where I'll hear the words "Well done, good and faithful servant! You have been faithful with a few things.... Come and share your master's happiness!" (Matthew 25:21).

Just a few things. Just a few.

I'm a Christian, but I'm a big fat doubter. And I have to be honest: there are times — a growing number of times — when I'd rather be a doubter than have it all figured out.

There. I said it.

About the Author

J ason Boyett is a blogger, writer, and speaker who lives in Amarillo, Texas. He is the author of several books, most notably the Pocket Guide series (including *Pocket Guide to the Apocalypse*, *Pocket Guide to the Afterlife*, and *Pocket Guide to the Bible*).

Jason has been featured on the History Channel and the National Geographic Channel and writes regularly about religion and popular culture. Follow Jason online at www.jasonboyett.com and twitter.com/jasonboyett.

Share Your Thoughts

With the Author: Your comments will be forwarded to the author when you send them to *zauthor@zondervan.com*.

With Zondervan: Submit your review of this book by writing to *zreview@zondervan.com*.

Free Online Resources at
www.zondervan.com

Zondervan AuthorTracker: Be notified whenever your favorite authors publish new books, go on tour, or post an update about what's happening in their lives at www.zondervan.com/authortracker.

Daily Bible Verses and Devotions: Enrich your life with daily Bible verses or devotions that help you start every morning focused on God. Visit www.zondervan.com/newsletters.

Free Email Publications: Sign up for newsletters on Christian living, academic resources, church ministry, fiction, children's resources, and more. Visit www.zondervan.com/newsletters.

Zondervan Bible Search: Find and compare Bible passages in a variety of translations at www.zondervanbiblesearch.com.

Other Benefits: Register yourself to receive online benefits like coupons and special offers, or to participate in research.

ZONDERVAN®

ZONDERVAN.com/
AUTHORTRACKER
follow your favorite authors